JOURNEY
By the Book

- a guide to tales of travel -

Daniel E. Van Tassel

Mechanicsburg, PA USA

Published by Sunbury Press, Inc.
Mechanicsburg, Pennsylvania

SUNBURY PRESS
www.sunburypress.com

FIRST SUNBURY PRESS EDITION: July 2022

Set in Adobe Garamond | Interior design by Crystal Devine | Cover by Ashley Nichole Walkowiak | Edited by Abigail Henson.

Publisher's Cataloging-in-Publication Data
Names: Van Tassel, Daniel E., author.
Title: Journey by the book : a guide to tales of travel / Daniel E. Van Tassel.
Description: First trade paperback edition. | Mechanicsburg, PA : Sunbury Press, 2022.
Summary: *Journey by the Book* focuses on works in which a voyage, pilgrimage, or journey is pivotal for the story's meaning and structure. It defines categories of travel literature, discusses the gamut of impulses prompting travel, travel writing and reading, and showcases narrative styles sure to stoke and satisfy a reader's wanderlust.
Identifiers: ISBN 978-1-62006-891-5 (softcover).
Subjects: TRAVEL / Special Interest / Literary | LITERARY CRITICISM / Comparative Literature | LITERARY CRITICISM / Books & Reading.

Product of the United States of America
0 1 1 2 3 5 8 13 21 34 55

Continue the Enlightenment!

Contents

Introduction: Exploring the Kingdom of Travel Literature 1

Steinbeck's America Revisited: *Travels with Charley* 22

Eric Newby's Mock-Epic Tale: A Short Walk in the Hindu Kush 28

Travels of Marco Polo 36

Ship Ahoy: Navigating *Gulliver's Travels* 41

Footprints in the Sand: Robyn Davidson Crossing the Australian Desert 48

Mark Twain Abroad 54

Following in Bunyan's Footsteps: *Pilgrim's Progress* 67

Jupiter Circles the Earth 74

Homer's *The Odyssey* 85

A Trip into the Congo: Penetrating the *Heart of Darkness* 90

A Guide to *On the Road* 95

Naipaul's Islamic Journey 101

Coleridge's *Rime of the Ancient Mariner* 107

Think and Ride at the Same Time: *Zen and the Art of Motorcycle Maintenance* 112

Adventures on the High Seas: Sailing the *Kon-Tiki* and *Round the World* with Captain Cook 119

Bryson's Expanded World: *A Walk in the Woods* 126

Dana "Before the Mast" 133

Traveling *Blue Highways* 142

On the Rails with Paul Theroux 148
Dare Take *The Lunatic Express*? 160
Epilogue 172
Descriptive Contents 174
Acknowledgments 183
Principal Works Cited 184
Permissions 186
About the Author 188

INTRODUCTION

- Exploring the Kingdom of Travel Literature -

From Homer's *Odyssey* to Steinbeck's *Travels with Charley*, people have whetted their wanderlust by reading, listening to, or plying their quills on tales of travel. A guide to travel literature, *Journey by the Book* seeks to prepare and resource both the would-be and the avid armchair traveler by focusing on selected works in which a voyage, pilgrimage, or journey is central to the work's meaning and structure. Comprising an introduction, twenty chapters highlighting outstanding travelogues, and an epilogue, the book is not so much a survey of travel tales as a guide to categories of travel literature and a focus on two-dozen eminently readable travel works.

My role as an author is that of a tour guide. Having visited the sites beforehand and by virtue of firsthand acquaintance with the various tales of travel discussed, I accompany and guide the reader, remarking on things to look for and keep in mind as the journey unfolds book by book. *Journey by the Book* is not an anthology. Rather, it is a collection of introductions to and critiques of choice volumes in the library of travel literature. The only samples or excerpts from the works surveyed are intermittent quotations and passages selected to illustrate observations made about the style, content, and themes distinctive to the tales. My purpose is to enable the reader as an armchair traveler to survey the kingdom of travel literature and become more aware of the infinite points of departure encompassed by tales of travel. The essays themselves comprise a multifaceted travelogue.

My primary aim in *Journey by the Book* is to stimulate and quench the thirst for travel (vicarious or actual) that is nearly universal and is shared by countless readers ready to venture to faraway places, book in hand. Veteran travelers will find both common ground as well as foreign territory. For the tyro traveler, it is hoped that the book will pique and nourish the appetite to sally forth on new adventures hither and yon. If the book leads its readers to peruse the very books it refers to and others like or different from them, it will have met the author's goal of expanding the ranks of would-be travelers. Our ticket to travel is a library membership, a digital text, or a stop at a bookstore, and our passage to other places is accommodated by a favorite lounge chair in a comfortable nook with a lamp or a sun-lit window to light the way. Bon voyage!

In an epistemological sense, all reading is synonymous with travel, for, in the activity of reading, our minds leave our present situation and depart for another. We embark, as it were, on a trip and pass the time learning, being entertained, and enlarging our world, crossing boundaries and returning refreshed, wiser, and more informed. The imagination, memory, mental powers, and educational skills facilitate the trip a reader takes by a book. By reading (or viewing in the case of art or film) another's depiction of a world different from ours, we make our own world much vaster and either better understood or increasingly mysterious.

In travel literature, the primary emphasis is on movement, time and space, our preoccupation with place, where we are heading, and what we encounter as we journey forth. The travel work may be preparing us for an actual trip, as in the case of a guidebook, or it may be informing us what we would experience were we actually—but while reading only vicariously—going there. In the company of the author, the guide, we progress on the way and join in and recreate the experience of the journey. Admittedly, the journey, not the destination, is the actual substance of the trip. Our pleasure derives from going more than simply arriving. The discussion includes works that have become journey classics, in which the journey motif, the book's itinerary, is more than an aspect of the setting. In such works, the setting is not merely background but looms into the foreground as a theme, at times virtually functioning as a sort of antagonist if not a protagonist. Like unfolding a complicated plot, the journey's narration grips hold of and entices the reader to keep going toward completion. Well-known works in which a journey motif is paramount include, for sure, Geoffrey Chaucer's *The Canterbury Tales*, Mark Twain's *Huck Finn*, Ernest Hemingway's *The Sun Also Rises* and *A Farewell to Arms*, Graham Greene's *The Power and the Glory*, and John Steinbeck's *The Grapes of Wrath*. The list goes on.

All novels feature settings that become new places to visit for the reader unfamiliar with the locale. However, the setting and geographical identity are of primary significance in some novels. Specifically, say, Spain in Hemingway's *The Sun Also Rises* and Italy in *A Farewell to Arms*; Egdon Heath in Hardy's *The Return of the Native*, the Dorset countryside in *Tess of the D'Urbervilles*, Christminster (aka Oxford) in *Jude the Obscure*, or Casterbridge (aka Dorchester) in *The Mayor of Casterbridge*; Mexico in Greene's *The Power and the Glory*; and Honduras in Theroux's *The Mosquito Coast*. In these and many other novels, the setting, far from being incidental or secondary, is critical to the characters' activities. In such works, the characters' relationships with the landscape become the defining factor.

In *Adventures of Huckleberry Finn*, the Mississippi River is essential to the plot and the theme of freedom. Huck, a well-intentioned lad, befriends Jim, a runaway slave. Their partnership as they float a raft south with the stream's current provides a string of humorous episodes and insights into moral issues and social and geographical phenomena. In a host of works, a quest or journey serves as the core of the book's development and meaning. Steinbeck's *The Grapes of Wrath* chronicles the westward migration undertaken as an escape from the dust bowl in the 30s, an epic struggle in America pitting families against hard times. The reader of a piece of fiction in which a journey is pivotal to the structure, plot, characterization, and theme of that work necessarily reckons with the setting as the story unfolds. The reader derives pleasure from participating in that journey and in the depiction of the dominant setting as its influence bears on the direction and outcome of the work as made manifest by the author's supreme control over it. The reader becomes engrossed in the journey, rapt by the direction it takes and the nature or state it assumes, and the purposes it appears to fulfill. As readers, we explore with the author as our guide and pathfinder.

In imaginary journey classics, such as *The Odyssey*, *Pilgrim's Progress*, *Gulliver's Travels*, and *The Rime of the Ancient Mariner*, the journey by the characters over water or across land, whether meandering or deliberate, constitutes a critical though fanciful feature without which the work and its import could not exist. In some works, the mode of travel defines the genre, as in Robert Louis Stevenson's *Travels with a Donkey*. Yet another variant is Ted Simon's *Jupiter's Travels*, a round-the-world trip on a motorcycle.

Or, shifting from a land journey to a voyage, take Frederic Doerflinger's *Slow Boat through England*, offering a guide to leisurely navigation on the rivers and old canals of Britain via "botels." The same holds for numerous parallel guides available for travel on luxury barges, cruise ships, sailboats, or canoes in and to many other countries. In this group belongs Richard Halliburton's *The Book of Marvels*. The traveler recounts a slew of exotic places where his signature Kilroy-was-here took the form of a swim, whether a dip in the pool at the Taj Mahal or a registered passage through the locks of the Panama Canal. Two other noteworthy works in the category are Thor Heyerdahl's *Kon-Tiki*, a voyage undertaken in the South Seas on a replicated raft, and Christian Beamish's *The Voyage of the 'Cormorant,'* a solitary voyage in a homemade sailboat off the coast of Baja.

The travel work may take us worldwide or, as in Douglas Adams' *The Hitchhiker's Guide to the Galaxy*, into outer space. As imagined in the novel, one can catch rides on interstellar ships and, with a computerized cosmic guidebook handy, zip from planet to planet in the great beyond of the infinite universe and, in the process, gain a strikingly unusual perspective on earthly entities. Or, as in the novel *Journey to the Centre of the Earth* by Jules Verne, the imaginary journey may penetrate the earth's surface and, spiraling downward in the shaft of a volcano, offer the explorers a chance to witness oddities and encounter adventures at every level. Or, as in Verne's *Twenty Thousand Leagues under the Sea*, the journey may involve a lengthy, adventure-steeped, and danger-fraught chase in a submarine after a behemoth of a sea creature, one which others had caught glimpses of before and which, worse than a reef, had caused shipwrecks and carnage. Another journey in the collection, *Around the World in Eighty Days,* chronicles a whirlwind race undertaken to make good on a boast. Under breathtaking constraints of the calendar and utilizing every available mode of transportation to relay the contestants from start to finish in record time—be it by boat, train, horse, elephant, balloon, sail-rigged sledge, or on foot—linking land and sea surfaces of the globe as expeditiously as possible, the journey ensures suspense. A consummate raconteur, Verne makes the make-believe believable, turning out page after page of the finest reportage, all masquerading as a minute-by-minute account of an actual trip but, in actuality, the brainchild of his imagination and store of knowledge. He rivals all masters of sci-fi stirred up in his wake. His books, while dazzling the reader with Olympian feats and Odyssean journeys, daringly mimic the possible. Therein lies the core of their appeal. Travel literature attests to the many and various routes the tellers take in their tales—adventure is an essential ingredient in all of them.

The picaresque tradition, pioneered in Spain by Cervantes' *Don Quixote* and perpetuated by English novelists Nash and, later, Smollett, Defoe, and Fielding, as well as continental novelists Le Sage and Stendhal, chronicles the antics, adventures, and derring-do of a rogue on the road (the so-called "picaro"). Authors of the picaresque hold up a mirror to reflect the colorful events, personages, and landscape encountered by the bold wayfarer on the highways and byways—or even, as in *Roderick Random*, on the high seas awash with pirates and desperadoes. The picaresque novel celebrates a string of rowdy episodes involving a narrator away from home. In the Renaissance and down through the centuries, when it was in vogue for English gentlemen to tour the Continent as part of their education and coming of age, the saying, "The Englishman itinerant is the devil incarnate," became popular, bearing on the theme of the traveler taking liberties and then back home imitating the ways of foreigners.

Early explorers deserve recognition. Not all adventurous sailors who set out to navigate uncharted seas, find new routes, and claim new lands published their findings. Thankfully, however, letters and diaries of some are extant. As with the journals that were printed and circulated more widely, these documents attest to the impulse of travelers to share their quest to discover and experience new places. Such accounts were designed not to guide others to follow so much as to report what they discovered and acknowledge, if not boast, that they made it there and back. Their patrons were often spurred on by the desire to propagandize and colonize. In this vein, much of what has come down to us has antiquarian value. The far-ranging ones that stand out are the travel accounts of Marco Polo and, later, Sir John Mandeville, Christopher Columbus, Ferdinand Magellan, Richard Hakluyt, Sir Francis Drake, and Captain Cook. Darwin's voyage on *HMS Beagle* in the 19th century explored a different venue of momentous importance for the basis of biology's unifying theory of evolution and natural selection. On land, Lewis and Clarke in the new continent and numerous explorers of the dark continent likewise kept refined journals for those back home.

Another source or type of travel literature is the memoir or quasi-autobiographical work that depends on a trip in time and space for its primary substance. Such works are hardly distinguishable from travelogues. In travelogues, the mode, method, destination, purpose, duration, and scope of the travel—all such matters of the journey—vary with the individual author's experience and intention. Bill Bryson's *Travels in Europe*, subtitled "Neither Here Nor There," and *The Lost Continent*, subtitled "Travels in Small-Town America," belong to the category best-termed travelogue. As do Paul Theroux's *The Great Railway Bazaar*, *The Old Patagonian Express*, and *Riding the Rooster*, three epic journeys by rail; his walking tour *Kingdom by the Sea: A Journey Around the Coast of Great Britain*; and his *The Happy Isles of Oceania*, subtitled "Paddling the Pacific." The travelogue differs from the travel guidebook in a specific way. Guidebooks are intended to show the way for the prospective traveler. In contrast, travelogues aim to content the armchair traveler, the person whose completion of the journey is coterminous with the completion of the book's reading.

The journey goes only that far, but that is sufficient. Most accounts of shared experience aren't designed to prompt readers to retrace the route celebrated in the account but, like jars of preserves on the shelf, are intended to retain the taste and harvest of a season. Samuel Johnson's trip to the Hebrides remains a daydream for the reader. It probably won't result in purchasing a single or roundtrip ticket by even the most enthusiastic reader. The companionship with Dr. Johnson and his biographer Boswell stays with the book. The reader's interest in Theroux, a contemporary travel writer whose works range from novels to travelogues, is not apt to increase the sale of tickets anywhere covered in what he has written, even though his readership is vast indeed. In such instances, the read happily serves as a surrogate for the go-to venture itself.

Then there are short pieces, works not in the same league as travelogues, lacking a full-scale itinerary and not composed to celebrate a journey to get somewhere. Such essays and chapters written by travelers sharing their views of a particular place—a city or state, a region, or some spot of interest—are available in magazines and newspapers, sometimes later appearing in a collection. In this category, for instance, belong *Locations* (1992) and *Journeys* (1984) by Jan Morris. Featured are verbal snapshots, equivalent to film clips, personalized and engraved in candid rather than posed vignettes. Morris's books contain chapter titles that take us straight to a place, as, for example: "A Visit to Barchester: Wells, England," "Fun City: Las Vegas, U.S.A.," "Trieste: Loitering on the Quay," "Canberra: Nothing if not Australian," Oaxaca: An Unquestionable Place," or "The Best of Everything: Stockholm, Sweden." In these write-ups, the author's proclaimed intention is to give a personal perspective. Not an encyclopedic description but something more spun out and chatty than a gazetteer; each piece is accorded the authenticity of a diarist's viewpoint, resembling the deliberately desultory character of a diary without the diary's customary neglect of pertinent research. When extended to a coherent journey connecting the cities and places surveyed separately, the narrative tips toward the travelogue genre and is brought closer to the domain of tales of travel, the part selected here for highest commendation. A variant of the narrowly focused short excursion, undertaken by diverse hands and edited by seasoned travel writers, is annually compiled in two paperback series: *The Best American Travel Writing* (New York: Houghton Mifflin Harcourt) and *The Best Travel Writing* (Palo Alto: Solas House).

In this ilk are Catherine Watson's *Home on the Road: Further Dispatches from the Ends of the Earth* (2007) and *Roads Less Traveled: Dispatches from the Ends of the Earth* (2005), both collections of columns previously published in the *Minneapolis Tribune*. On separate trips for short lengths of time, we bounce around from place to place, from one continent and a country or state to another. Among her closeups are the family cabin in northern Minnesota, a home away from home in Easter Island, several stops in the British Isles, including a remote village in Scotland, a glimpse into the Newfoundland of the Vikings of old, the tale of enduring Shakers, the incident of a scorpion bite in Costa Rica, and other sojourns of personal significance. The 2007 volume features trips to the Himalayas, the Falklands, Peru, Mexico, Canada, and elsewhere. Always up for new departures and activities, she tells of driving through Death Valley in a station wagon sans air-conditioning, dog-sledding in northern Minnesota, riding the restored Orient Express in July from London to Venice, celebrating the Day of the Dead in Mexico, surviving a harrowing adventure aboard a raft on the Colorado rapids deep in the Grand Canyon, and navigating the Amazon, the north-flowing Mackenzie, and a variety of foreign seas. An accomplished photographer, Watson loaded film in her camera and jotted notes in her diary on a safari in Tanzania. On another trip, she recorded observations in the wake of Darwin's explorations and findings in the Galapagos. She often uses apt, occasionally even photogenic comparisons to buttress her observations. One such instance involves her description of the icebergs off the north Atlantic coast, catching a view of multiple icebergs just as the clouds disperse. Varied in sentence design and vocabulary, sparked now and again by a nicely picked simile or metaphor, and replete with pertinent detail, her style is compelling. For our purposes, however, the miscellaneous accounts do not hew to a single sustained journey and lack a developing rapport between narrator and reader.

So too with Larry McMurtry, novelist and screenwriter, whose *Roads: Driving America's Great Highways* (2000) covers a lot of ground, some cement, more blacktop, and, endearingly, even dirt, especially as it borders his homestead. The dirt roads around the Texas ranch where he grew up take the prize for writer and reader alike. The memories flood and recede, swell and subside, offsetting the marathon drives that occur at intervals and crisscross other roads taken earlier or yet to be driven. Like *Blue Highways*, the book eschews the freeways in favor of lesser, more interesting roads and concentrates on a solitary driver-narrator. *Roads*, by design, has no fixed itinerary and is not a single journey. The book tangentially biographies the author, primarily focusing on his youth and his father's influence that begat his early interest in driving, and defines and provides intriguing bits of history and colorful detail about large parts of the U.S.A.

Mined from a slightly different vein are such travelogues as historian Arnold Toynbee's *East to West: A Journey Round the World* (1958). While fulfilling the requirement of narrating a continuous trip, piecing together cities, countryside, landmasses, and oceans, Toynbee's work does not reach a personalized account of a journey involving encounters, often turning into friendships, with other persons. His are generalized portraits of a farmer, a Muslim, a host, and the women in the village. Close-ups of ruins, lakes, busy ports, pyramids, airstrips and railways, mosques and other buildings of distinctive architecture, rice paddies, and geographical wonders abound. Apt historical and literary allusions and pensive glimpses of scenes enriched by legend or transformed by modern technology—there is much here to please and inform the would-be traveler. But the reader looks in vain for a personalized tale of travel like that narrated by a Richard Dana, a Ted Simon, a Paul Theroux, or a Bill Bryson. In Toynbee, the description focuses on buildings and features of the land. He proffers sweeping views of those who inhabit the land with due attention to historical and political facts underlying the nations and capitals visited. Herds of elephants and indigenous populations stand out as snapshots in an album. His account closes a bit wistfully, acknowledging its concentration on cities to the neglect of broader, non-urban habitations. The writing is lucid and informative, frequently insightful, but lacks the element of adventure and the virtue of a connected vision of humanity.

For an inverse of Toynbee, take V. S. Pritchett's *The Offensive Traveller* (1964), titled *Foreign Faces* when published in England. The collection of essays originally appearing separately in the magazine *Holiday* over a period extending over half a dozen years fails to convey the sense of a continuous journey. Granted, its narrator is chatty and insightful, meets and brings to life many interesting individuals, and describes intimately, with wit and verve, the various places he visits, from countries in Eastern Europe, to cities in Spain, to Turkey and Iran in the Middle East. He's a person whose company the reader adores. Yet this is not a tale of travel *per se*. Instead, it is a string of short accounts of distant places visited told by a charismatic teller in a captivating style, absent the concept of an overarching journey. But enough to indicate what we are highlighting by the rubric "Tales of Travel."

The travel books extolled here narrate a journey during which they typically feature stopping points, brief or extended, but keep moving along, emphasizing the journey itself and, concomitantly, what the traveler encounters and reflects upon en route. All lingering is temporary; the onward march of the itinerary is paramount. The scope is more comprehensive than a selected city, province, or island whose identity and character are studied and delineated as the sole, concentrated focus. Granted, the stipulated borders become slightly blurred, somewhat artificial, in our differentiating a journey narrative from a travelogue centering on a given locale (as in the case of Defoe's *Robinson Crusoe* or D. H. Lawrence's *Sea and Sardinia* or, as even more pronounced, Frances Trollope's *Domestic Manners of the Americans*). The touchstone is scale, whether the trip is of larger magnitude, duration, and significance than a mere one-stop-get-there-and-back-again event. For definition and inclusion, targeted works in *Journey by the Book* are tales of travel distinguished by narrative appeal, which subsumes the descriptive element. The most important qualification is that the work engenders and sustains an irresistible rapport between the reader and the narrator by dint of its style. In works of the highest-ranking the descriptive and meditative quality of the text and the presence of a continuous journey complement the chemistry of writer and reader, traveler and accompanying armchair traveler. Finally, literary excellence is the requisite criterion for predicating a work of travel a genuine travelogue and, at the highest level, a tale of travel. Based on the superior quality of the writing, whether fine prose or verse, the work can rightfully be termed belletristic. Devoid of commercial bias and possessing the defining marks of the travelogue genre—narrative mode, felicity of language, and the journey dynamic—a work achieves status as a tale of travel.

A case in point are the travel books of Freya Stark. Her works dealing with the Middle East and the northern Mediterranean, including *The Zodiac Arch*, *Iona: A quest*, *The Valley of the Assassins*, *Beyond Euphrates*, and *The Arab Island*, do not depict continuous journeys but rather are compilations of discrete essays on aspects of particular cultures. While Stark offers thoughtful and detailed accounts, so much has changed in the geographical portions of her concentration that the topical and ephemeral have nearly eclipsed the ongoing appeal for both armchair and real-time traveler wishing to visit those parts of the world. Albeit eminently readable, nicely documented treatises, theirs is a reduced legacy of historical and anthropological—if not also literary—merit.

* * *

In another nook in the library of travel are shelves devoted to guidebooks. They aim to prepare the traveler to go to particular places, often on a given route, by providing pertinent information on sights to visit, lodging and dining options, what to pack and not pack, and preferred modes and times of travel. They tell the tourist what to do and what not to do. From the classic old-world series by Baedekers and the later Blue Guides to the popular guidebooks and videos of Rick Steves, from the budget-minded Frommer's *Europe on Five* and its price-conscious sequels to the name-dropping Michelin guides for the affluent, Cook's tour guides intended for those in between, or the vanguard guides of The Lonely Planet—the production of guidebooks appeals to all categories of would-be or will-be travelers. Enticing, well-illustrated articles in issues of *Conde Nast*, *National Geographic Travel*, *Travel + Leisure*, and *AFAR* serve a slice of the market for travel guides. Often, they explore fetching travel options. Some claim to have spotted the ultimate dining experience and fashion shopping or the perfect getaway for privacy.

Among the bountiful crop of guidebooks is a strain dedicated to a single locality, region, state, or country. Bookshelves of specialized travel guides proliferate, some of the more ephemeral appearing in annuals and bookstores everywhere. For the traveler sojourning in the British Isles, there are choices galore: for the landlubber mariner, the aforementioned *Slow Boat through England*; for the walker, Reginald Hammond's *The Lake District* (from the Ward Lock series), *Country Walks* (one of the scores of guidebooks available from London Transport), Eric Delderfield's *Travel with Me: The Story of a Journey through the English Countryside, of Places, People and Memories*, or *A Book of Wales*, an anthology devoted to Wales, chock full of excerpts from poems and prose works by authors celebrating facets of Welsh life and romance and the glory of its landscapes and legends. Heinrich Böll's *Irish Journal*, now quite dated, gives an outsider's view of the land and people of the Emerald Isle. Add arcane titles, some new, some old, like *Skating to Antarctica*, *Slowly Down the Ganges*, and *The Romany Rye*, and—presto!—the library expands globally. We ought not to leave undisturbed the sleepers whose titles conceal any peregrinating. Consider the singular George Borrow's *The Bible in Spain*. Far from being a ledger of copies of Holy Writ purveyed in the early 19th century, the book is a fascinating, elaborately carved log by an accomplished novelist. In strokes characterized by a decidedly sesquipedalian style, he paints a detailed picture of the tumultuous times and the dangerous twists and adventures that befell him as he rode astride his Arabian stallion across the land. The multiplicity of subjects for guidebooks is phenomenal. Published in 2021, *World Traveler: An Irreverent Guide*, by Anthony Bourdain (posthumously) and co-author Laurie Woolever, erstwhile chef, assistant, and "lieutenant," as he tagged her, is a specialized travel guide for those with a discerning palate and a hankering for adventures in cross-cultural dining. A sequel to *Appetites* (2016), it fills the bill for a cult. Stops around the planet include sites in forty-three countries, with considerable emphasis on American cuisine. The book may prove a boon for well-heeled post-pandemic travelers and less-moneyed armchair ruminators excited to explore the reopening of foreign ports of call to indulge palate-pleasing ways via a guide book smacking of authority and targeted appeal.

Guidebooks typically are more expository and descriptive than narrative. They are designed to resource their readers for specialized travel. They can result in write-ups about the experience their users had by pursuing recommendations offered by the particular book in hand. Published by Mountaineers Books in 2021, *Hut to Hut USA: The Complete Guide for Hikers, Bikers, and Skiers* is co-authored by Sam Demas and Laurel Bradley, both academics, one a librarian emeritus and the other a former curator of an art museum, at a small, prestigious Midwestern liberal arts college. For its hearty users, the book showcases eighteen places in the continental United States that offer a comprehensive setup of three or more "huts" (i.e., facilities with beds, toilets, and cook-yourself kitchens or prepared meals) as well as the availability of pertinent sports equipment (by rent or purchase) and desired amenities. Situated at higher elevations of stunning recreational and environmental appeal, they range in location from Mount Tahoma in Washington to the Adirondacks and Appalachians in the Northeast. Chock full of information, the book includes details on making reservations and what to expect in costs. Info regarding logistics, sample itineraries, topographical maps, and colorful photos fill up its pages.

* * *

Among books that serve as starting points for *Journey by the Book*, in that they explore the origins, cite examples, and note categories of travel literature and would therefore be of interest to the armchair traveler, is Paul Fussell's anthology *The Norton Book of Travel* (1987). The book provides a lively introductory essay and brief orientations to the sections and individual selections that follow. It is a kaleidoscope of travel literature, with colorful bits and pieces, both ancient and modern. On the American front, Twain, Hemingway, and Kerouac are represented by excerpts, and several others are briefly included. Of course, much has since appeared in travel literature exploring the USA.

More recently, Paul Theroux, in *The Tao of Travel: Enlightenments from Lives on the Road* (2011), revisits the library of travel literature to assess its legacy and promise for the future. It is less an anthology than a potpourri, a collection of quotations—some annotated, others not, and ranging in length from one to two paragraphs to a few pages—organized to illustrate aspects of travel and drawn from scores of writers down through the ages and across the globe, including plentiful examples from Theroux's canon. The book testifies to the positive and negative aspects of traveling, whether in actuality or vicariously as armchair travelers. It encompasses innumerable points of departure and succeeds in whetting the appetite to travel and read about travels. Topics covered include exotic foods, downsides and upsides of travel, faraway places, sage advice, traveling companions, modes of travel, phony accounts, moods or disorders peculiar to travelers, and odd baggage.

The book in hand considers some of the same American authors encompassed in the Norton anthology and the output of more recent travel writers—Steinbeck, Pirsig, Heat-Moon, and Bryson, to mention four who recite journeys across America. The present book is not intended to be a comprehensive survey of travel literature, a touch-up-on-everything, dwell-upon-nothing volume. Nor is it a tome of scholarly nature, plowing entirely new ground and offering copious notes and an extensive list of works consulted. It is not an anthology either. And it doesn't aim to serve as a history of travel literature. Such surveys are plentiful, among the more notable being Peter Hulme and Tim Youngs, eds., *The Cambridge Companion to Travel Writing* (2002), especially Part I, and Jás Elsner and Joan-Pau Rubiés, *Voyages and Visions: Towards a Cultural History of Travel* (1999). *Journey by the Book* primarily attempts to ignite and sustain interest in travel literature, encouraging inquisitive readers to pick and choose titles that appeal to them, just as place names on a map fascinate the latent traveler in us all as we pore over possibilities for expanding our horizons. *Journey* is idiosyncratic to the extent that the works mentioned and those discussed in detail resonate with me, the author and guide.

The Cambridge History of English and American Literature (2009), under the heading "The Literature of Travel," nicely demarks two kinds or classes of travel accounts. One class comprises texts by persons whose profession is regarded as more of a writer than a traveler per se. This set constitutes the higher echelon of travel literature. Accounts of the second type, the corollary, are texts written by persons mainly seeking to render a faithful account or transcribe a diary of a particular travel event. Presumably, they made little or no attempt to achieve literary status but were chiefly motivated to render a trustworthy report. Consisting largely of published records of explorers and discoverers, this second set might usefully be labeled documentaries and historical records. Such accounts inherently excite interest by the lore they convey and the distances and modes the respective chroniclers traveled and advanced the frontiers of space and time. Their primary worth lies in the information they contain, often of scientific merit and serving as a foundation for further study, verification, and elaboration. They address facts and tend to eschew fiction. They traffic more in the accuracy of detail and straightforward prose, with scant reliance on figurative language. The persona and outlook of the recorder are not in the forefront as they are in what can be readily identified as the literature of travel. *Journey by the Book* celebrates the former while acknowledging the latter.

I especially like and find apt the definition of travel literature offered by Christopher Brown in his *Encyclopedia of Travel Literature* (2000). As he studies the ins and outs, travel literature includes texts wherein travel is the focal point, both as the celebrated event and as the targeted subject of interpretation and reflection. For him and us, we can expect each text in the top echelon of travel literature to portray differences between phenomena in the place being explored and phenomena back home and to convey the narrator's rationale for making judgments about such similarities and differences. With this classification, the purpose is not to build fences but to open gates and invite passage across boundaries. Most literary works, especially those that appeal widely, defy strict labeling. They transcend efforts to pin them down to a single genre or type. A work that constitutes a period piece and is tagged by its locale may arguably as well rise to the universal, liberated from any facile pigeon-holing. While the tales of travel encompassed in *Journey*, imagined and actual journeys alike, cover the globe and span the ages, exemplifying the definition we are setting here, many of these signal works chronicle trips in or across the USA.

Annotated lists—pick the number eighty-six, 100, or higher—of the greatest travel books ever, and collections and catalogs of travel books by year or by country of origin are readily available online. *Journey by the Book* is an invitation to roam the shelves of travel literature to encounter and welcome new vistas, thereby expanding, even reprioritizing, the list of each reader's favorites. Everybody loves to go or return to remarkable places.

Travel sections in bookstores typically feature a raft of special focus books and maps and a stocked cupboard to feed the wanderlust of the would-be armchair traveler. The curious reader-traveler can locate choice volumes, maybe Patricia Schultz's immensely popular *1,000 Places to See Before You Die*, a title playing on the adage "See Naples and Die." Travel literature collectively features an inexhaustible variety of modes of travel, all of which are managed vicariously by the reader. This polyatholon stays in place while going by the book.

In the case of established writers, their travel is pursued expressly to publish an account—the journal and notes of things observed serving as grist. In this sense, the published manuscript becomes the writer's souvenir. The traveler whose incentive for traveling is to gather raw material for a book is equally eager to indulge in the pleasure of travel and to keep a running commentary, which upon return will be finished and turned into the written narration to be submitted for publication. The writer's ore is the travel; the book is the pure metal extracted. Such is the alchemy of tales of travel.

Who, why, how, where, when, and for how long? The combination of these factors, the formula, in brief, defines the uniqueness of the journey; written out in length, the travel book's purpose is to guide the journey in its retelling. Just as travel is generally regarded as a way to expand one's knowledge and refresh and enrich one's life, reading a work premised on travel and uncovering an unusual setting can enhance one's grasp of geography and culture without moving a foot. The educational value of leaving one's homeland and traveling and sojourning in other countries is epitomized in "the grand tour" undertaken by students back in the day and in the longstanding and ongoing practice of studying abroad for a term.

* * *

As a fellow traveler, allow me a brief history of my circuitous route to the present book. Among my earliest travel recollections are trips we made as a family, foremost a trip to Denver and the top of Pikes Peak, stopping every so many hairpin curves to cool the motor and add water to the radiator of Dad's 1947 Chevrolet and to take photos with Mom's Brownie camera. Other outings that vie for memory space are a two-hour road trip to Crystal Cave in Spring Valley, Wisconsin, to study differences between stalactites and stalagmites, and repeated drives of similar duration to Minneapolis or, less often, to Stillwater, to visit relatives and shop in the city. Lingering fondly in my album of memories are short—well, *long* for a carload of fidgety children—rides to a cottage on nearby Prairie Lake in Chetek to spend a week or weekend in the summer fishing, swimming, boating, and enjoying primitive life. Snapshots from the past flash images of an outdoor, two-holer biffy, a pump in the kitchen that had to be primed to start water flowing, a genuine icebox, a wood-burning stove, and four substantial beds cozily covered with colorful, tufted quilts and all in a row on a large enclosed porch-cum-addition to the original one-room cabin.

Another category of remembered trips involves getaways our parents took (by themselves or with friends) to places such as Toronto and Castle Loma, New York and the Empire State Building, and Niagara Falls. Once, with friends, they went off to the Ozarks for sightseeing and relaxation and a couple of times to northern Minnesota to fish and, I'm sure, swat mosquitoes. Regarding *their* trips, my travel was secondhand rather than firsthand. Back then, it was, as it still is, difficult to distinguish between actual participation, those times when the whole family traveled together, and the times when we children reviewed postcards, photographs, and slides of a trip our parents took. It was as if we shared the trip; we became so familiar with the sights and experiences they let us in on. We did not feel the urge to duplicate those trips for real on our own later on, content with the details caught in picture form or recreated in our minds from descriptions given by the returned travelers themselves, our parents.

Yet another set of early recollections springs from reading tales of travel. Works that appealed to my fledgling wanderlust and had me migrating to other climates, places, and times were the missionary routes of the Apostle Paul, the story of Joseph in Egypt, and other biblical narratives read or told in Sunday School and Daily Vacation Bible School, often enriched by flannelgraph illustrations. Like dreams partially forgotten, the good old stories supplemented by adventure tales set in remote parts of the world—Little Black Sambo in Africa, Hans Brinker in Holland, Tiny Tim in London, Alice in Wonderland, and Sinbad the Sailor—offered a curriculum I was eager to learn and would never forget.

During college and for decades following, I took trips by road, air, and rail. Traveling with various friends, colleagues, and family members, or sometimes solo or hitchhiking, I experienced and validated sites stretching from the Pacific to the Atlantic. Places visited included mountain ranges noted for breath-taking vistas and challenging ski slopes, national parks and state capitals, museums of all sorts, monuments right out of American history books and featured in gazetteers. Like fossils in a natural history museum and more telltale than fingerprints, we have collections of predominantly travel-oriented postcards, letters, diaries, photos, albums, and slides in closets and a spare room. Mementos yet to be sorted and ultimately put to rest, such artifacts comprise a montage, gallimaufry, or cluttered still-life concealing stories of bygone days that, as in Keats's "Grecian Urn," come to life again when closely viewed by an active imagination coupled with memory.

When my wife and I were newly married, we spent a summer traveling in Europe in a rented Citroen 2CV. Flying BOAC, we refueled in Reykjavik, Iceland and landed in Prestwick, Scotland. En route to Glasgow, we paused to behold the engineering marvel of the suspension bridge spanning the Firth of Forth. We were introduced to roundabouts and goodly instances of Scottish warmth. The driver of a lorry who gave us a lift from the airport called our attention to a park, which he termed "the city's lungs, ye know, the breathin' spaces of the city." Edinburgh, in the awakening of early May, heartily welcomed us. We strolled down glorious Princes Street, tramped up to Arthur's Seat and the Palace of Holyrood, and visited the Castle to take in the droning bagpipes of kilted Scotsmen performing a "Tattoo" on the Esplanade. Later, we stopped to revere John Knox's gravesite, sorted out the tartan of my wife's heritage at the Museum of Antiquities, and enjoyed a leisurely morning in the fragrant, colorful Botanical Garden.

The sights, sounds, and smells out and about capped off a cozy stay at a B&B. Treated to tea and scones upon arriving and before retiring each night handed "a wee bottle" of hot water "tah warm ye bed" and linger after the shilling's worth of heat from the gas fireplace had expired, we felt like royalty. Our reign included British breakfasts. Just prior to beginning our driving tour of the Highlands, we gained advice from an elderly Scotsman who happened to be tramping along the road where our auto was stopped while we studied the map to determine the most promising road to engage. To our query as to which of the routes we were fingering on the map would be most scenic, he replied in splendid brogue, "Ah, it's all bonnie land!" He was right. It was a picture book from Loch Ness and Urquhart Castle to the gorse-clad hills and flocks of shaggy sheep crossing the road.

As we journeyed through the British Isles and onto the Continent on a budget guided by Frommer's *Europe on Five*, we pleased ourselves with the daily novelty of sustaining life without the aid of the supermarket. Likewise, picnic-like living conditions with provisions bought at local bakeries and green-grocers prevailed on later trips and stays in England.

Our teaching careers were punctuated by study tours, research trips, and teaching opportunities abroad. I designed and conducted a series of study tours that I dubbed "Literary Haunts of the British Isles" and offered students as an attractive alternative to the fleet of on-campus interim courses. Building on such sorties and partnering with a colleague from another institution, a history professor, we helped inaugurate a Semester-in-England program sponsored by and drawing students from a consortium of private colleges and universities in the Pacific Northwest. Moreover, my scholarly interests in Thomas Hardy led to interludes of research at libraries with germane holdings, notably the Dorset County Museum, the main repository for autograph Hardy correspondence. Then, during a teaching term in London, our daughter Abigail began her elementary education in an infant-primary school in Highgate, just a few blocks away from our flat and a handy Northern Line tube stop. My experience living and traveling abroad was further buttressed by a stint as academic dean, during which I formed and fostered a unique network of one-for-one exchange arrangements for studying and teaching abroad. Students and faculty simply swapped places with their respective counterparts on the host campuses at the cost of only a roundtrip flight. The program linked a small traditional liberal arts college in Ohio with universities in countries and territories as diverse and far-flung as Canada, Mexico, Puerto Rico, China, Hong Kong, Japan, Taiwan, Germany, Ireland, England, Scotland, Spain, France, Greece, Costa Rica, Australia, and Brazil. It proved an exhilarating yet thrifty way for students and faculty to be issued passports to global understanding and citizenship.

Another radius of my circle of travel experience draws from creating a special course, christened "Tales of Travel," various versions of which I taught over the years. Call it rationalization, but I believe my literary interest has nicely blended with my wanderlust. To travelers bound for England, I heartily recommend a book by Ruth McKenney and Richard Bransten. Beckoningly entitled *Here's England* and alluringly subtitled "A Highly Informal Guide," first published by Harper in 1950, it wonderfully bridges the two great sources of enjoyable learning—reading and traveling (or reading about traveling).

* * *

But enough background. Suffice it to say that the impetus for the book in hand is a longstanding interest in travel, both first- and secondhand. Now it's time to depart, to delve into books that invite us to travel to faraway places. Each book is a ticket and offers a distinct itinerary. Welcome aboard!

First, a word while on the gangplank before the anchor is pulled and the vessel recedes from the shore. The list of stops, the table of contents, warrants a notice. Our ports of call are ambitious but not exhaustive. Of course, space constraints and judgment calls enter the equation, for the sheer number of travelogues available necessitates the exclusion of many. The order of consideration reflected in the table of contents, our itinerary, is not based on dates of composition nor the time frame of the settings for the respective journeys. Neither is the book arranged into sections by countries traversed. The order of titles getting a close look is not alphabetical by authors, nor is it grouped according to whether the journey is imaginary or involves an actual route taken. The sequence laid out is purposefully varied. Discussions of imaginary journeys flip-flop with those of actual (or presumably factual) journeys. Modes by which the travels are undertaken and time frames and places comprising the respective settings of the tales are likewise deliberately mixed. Another elastic is the relative length of chapters, with deliberate alternation of longer and shorter ones for ease of pace. Quite apart from the order set by the table of contents, however, the choice of order in which chapters are read is clearly up to the reader, there being no necessity to follow the sequence as presented. Readers, like their traveling counterparts, are invited and encouraged to go whichever direction they please.

Now is a good time to point out that among a ship's papers, the equivalent typically being sequestered in the "End Matter" of a book, are navigation documents and paraphernalia that can influence the direction and success of the voyage. In addition to a bibliography, acknowledgement, permission pages featured in the so-called end matter, there is a descriptive or annotated chapter-by-chapter table of contents. A reference tool, the expanded contents (or log) can serve either as a convenient review (to look back and assess the wake) or as a preview (to chart the preferred course ahead). Essentially, it functions as a glorified index or itinerary of the unfolding journey. Unless, after poring over the expanded contents, the reader-traveler of *Journey* opts to depart for another port of call than that designated as the initial one in the itinerary, namely Steinbeck's *Travels with Charley*, that reader is set to sail and can start turning the pages of the desired chapter. Later on, should the reader zigzagging along at any point become a bit road weary or temporarily OD on waves and wish to switch to a different mode of travel, say, exchange sea legs for a tramp or ditch the road and get aboard a train or plane, that reader-traveler is at liberty simultaneously to satisfy a craving and resume the route underway. Conveniently, train and bus stations, airports, ferry docks and cruise ship ports, crossroads, and diverging trails abound around the globe! A compass or GPS tracker, maps, and travel books offer a plethora of directions to head. With *Journey by the Book,* the armchair traveler is handed the advantages of being accompanied, guided, and inspired on the way.

STEINBECK'S AMERICA REVISITED

- Travels with Charley -

Steinbeck's epic saga in Grapes of Wrath, when destitute farmers in the dust bowl headed west to seek relief, gave way to happier sequels in the narratives of others who crossed the country and fulfilled their dreams of discovering and sharing all that America offers. Steinbeck, too, later retraces and enlarges his itinerary across America. His *Travels with Charley*, Kerouac's *On the Road*, Pirsig's *Zen and the Art of Motorcycle Maintenance*, and Heat-Moon's *Blue Highways*, to call out the names of a few, all sing verses of Dinah Shore's once immensely popular "See the USA in your Chevrolet." Riverboats, trains, and all manner of terrain vehicles, from Conestoga wagons and stagecoaches to automobiles, trucks, motorcycles, jeeps, and busses plying the trails, roads, and highways and rails crisscrossing the nation, pointed and transported Americans the way west. Cruising at great speed and radically cutting travel and sight-seeing time, airplanes joined the parade, soaring overhead and pursuing their passes high above the clouds, mountains, fields, rivers, and network of roads below. Traveling across the Continental Divide became more accessible. Of course, the nature of the adventure changed with each different mode of travel and with each traveler and any who accompanied. America changed as the nation became settled. Thanks to Teddy Roosevelt, John Muir, and other champions of unmolested space, national parks were established to hold on to large portions of wilderness and preserve the plants, animals, and landscapes. The Eisenhower legacy of an interstate highway system speeded up traffic. However, it homogenized America in the process, especially with the advent and proliferation of franchises, which, ironically, at the same time obliterated a lot of what travelers set out on vacations to photograph and experience. Postcards, verbal and written travel accounts, films, and other pictorial media have endlessly documented scenes of the country and given stereoscopic closeness to remote and famous spots throughout the land.

When Steinbeck reached retirement age, he decided he needed to rediscover the country he had not traversed in recent years. He wanted to witness and record the changes big and little that inevitably had occurred in his absence. A world traveler, he felt compelled to renew his domestic citizenship. Raised in California, he had spent a good share of his life in New York and had done a fair amount of globetrotting. The subtitle of the book he produced, *In Search of America*, identifies the journey's purpose: defining what constitutes the nationhood; its citizens, its accomplishments, its towns, its way of life, the outlook and language of its people as modified by their backgrounds and the parts of the country they lived and grew up in; the sweep and varying contour of the landscape; and the striking range of climates and regions. He set out to delineate the character of American life in the 60s. He sought to answer the question, "'What are Americans like today?'" (185). Bolstered by firsthand encounters, arriving incognito in the company of Charley Dog, and traveling together in a made-to-order camper pickup that served as a "turtle shell" (6), the author-journalist dug into the American soil with a pen as his spade. In a celebratory mood, he dubbed his rig Rocinante in honor of the steed ridden by the inventor of the picaresque novel.

Steinbeck's discovery was twofold: wilderness places were still accessible, but modern throw-away society had encroached conspicuously. "American cities," he observed, "are like badger holes, ringed with trash—all of them—surrounded by wrecked and rusting automobiles, and almost smothered with rubbish" (22). He saw way too much litter and waste. He was appalled by the heavy vehicular traffic he encountered in cities. But clearly, he has fun mentioning the impact on him of traffic. In the thick of it in the Twin Cities, he laments figuratively,

> As I approached, a great surf of traffic engulfed me, waves of station wagons, rip tides of roaring trucks. . . . First the traffic struck me like a tidal wave and carried me along, a bit of shiny flotsam bounded

> in front by a gasoline truck half a block long. Behind me was an enormous cement mixer on wheels, its big howitzer revolving as it proceeded. On my right was what I judged to be an atomic cannon. As usual I panicked and got lost. Like a weakening swimmer I edged to the right into a pleasant street only to be stopped by a policeman, who informed me that trucks and such vermin were not permitted there. He thrust me back into the ravening stream (99-100).

Undaunted, he keeps going on his adventure and revs up his account of it. "I drove for hours, never able to take my eyes from the surrounding mammoths. I must have crossed the river but I couldn't see it. I never did see it. I never saw St. Paul or Minneapolis. All I saw was a river of trucks; all I heard was a roar of motors. The air saturated with Diesel fumes burned in my lungs. Charley got a coughing fit and I couldn't take time to pat him on the back" (100). Finally, he gets on the Evacuation Route, which leads him to fantasize over the apocalypse that the designers of the escape road must have had in mind when they built a way for people to exit if and when a bomb were to be dropped on this urban civilization. Unfortunately, the shell-shocked driver isn't cheered up by the stop he makes at a restaurant, once out of the near mayhem and Mayday traffic, for it was a flop in both menu and service. However, the dialogue and description of the occupants and staff go a long way toward crossing out the negatives.

When off the main road and away from natural stimulating hiatuses, Steinbeck found that he learned most by visiting casually with locals. He "discovered that if a wayfaring stranger wishes to eavesdrop on a local population the places for him to slip in and hold his peace are bars and churches" (27). Like Heat-Moon, who eschewed franchises in preference for local cafes, Steinbeck took refuge in "the roadside restaurant where men gather for breakfast before going to work or going hunting" (28). Not that conversation was forthcoming. He noted, "Early-rising men not only do not talk much to strangers, they barely talk to one another. Breakfast conversation is limited to a series of laconic grunts. The natural New England taciturnity reaches its glorious perfection at breakfast" (28). Even the lack of talk told him much about a breed of Americans and their vernacular.

Steinbeck's trip taught him a lot he didn't know about his native land. It was a field trip that educated both the traveler and the reader. One tidbit relates to the nation's agriculture: "There are three great potato-raising sections—Idaho, Suffolk County on Long Island, and Aroostook, Maine" (47). The statistics of potatoes grown astounded him, as did the numerous ways to prepare potatoes. He documents certain extremes with clarity and obvious consternation, for instance, his surprise over finding that a lot more racial prejudice and narrow world views existed than he had supposed.

As part of the business of traveling, Steinbeck differentiates types of travelers. Some, he says, spend more time poring over maps than gazing at the world beyond the windshield, paying attention to the routes they are following rather than the phenomena and customs peculiar to the region they are visiting and, one would suppose, not merely passing through. Adventurous others are wide awake to the novelties and irregularities they run across, not being shackled by a rigid schedule or preset itinerary. He looks beyond the road for signs of real life.

Steinbeck's trip turned out to be a Rip Van Winkle wake-up experience. Springing up during his absence, and thus new to him, were the frequent roadside rest stops with their trademark deodorized lavatories and well-stocked vending machines, the count-on-it standardized restaurants, and the endless panoply of available packaged goods, including a gamut of hygienic amenities for refreshing truckers and other exhausted wayfarers. Steinbeck awoke to the ubiquitous mobile home community. At first glance, he acknowledged it as a wave of novelty, but then he was hit with nausea over the glut and monotony of it all. Additionally, the trip reinforced and aggravated his distaste for a non-sustainable way of life, a society given to discarding and pursuing sameness on a colossal scale, heading he guesses for doom.

In tales of travel, the journey is largely the narrator's perception of how things differ or resemble things closer to home. One experience of the traveler that Steinbeck registers is that of the sudden feeling of remoteness caused when a momentary connection occurs with the part of the world temporarily eclipsed by the traveler's involvement in the journey, the traveler's preoccupation with a place and time different from that at home. A letter, email, or phone call bringing news from home—in this instance, a call from his wife, who would meet him at such a time and place in Texas to visit friends—can melt the distance that travel succeeds in solidifying. Such is the case when near the end of his motorcycle tour around the world, Simon, in *Jupiter's Travels*, interrupts his journey briefly to fly home to attend his father's funeral and to comfort his mother. The telegram puts India on hold and thrusts London into the forefront.

Places, the stuff of a journey, invariably impact the traveler. In Steinbeck's *Travels*, the section about the Midwest is almost an idyll. Wisconsin is "a noble land of good fields and magnificent trees, a gentleman's countryside, neat and white-fenced" (97). But that fond depiction is quickly qualified by realizing that much of the bounty, or control of the bounty, is due to government subsidies and mandates. As expected on any trip, Steinbeck's trip has highs and lows. Some towns and cities get kudos; some places get low ratings. Fargo is secure in the legend of possessing the most extreme climate, being "blizzard-riven, heat-blasted, dust-raddled" (105). Texas, which proved to be "a state of mind," "an obsession" (173), almost "a religion" (174), offers its guests—Steinbeck and his wife and his dog, no exception—entertainment and variety, culminating in a Thanksgiving "orgy" (179). But it is ultimately Montana that he falls "in love with" (121). Had the states or territories he visited vied for prizes at a state fair, it's no secret that Judge Steinbeck would have awarded Montana a sky-blue ribbon, Texas a deep red one, and the Midwest a bright white one. If Steinbeck were alive today and could revisit cities he took in while traveling with Charley, he would be pleased to see how urban renewal and a shift to the historic core have restored many of them to the level of life and attraction he felt had departed. He enjoyed tramping along Seattle's waterfront, but he deplored the changes occurring in the inner city there and elsewhere, as activity and population receded to the outskirts, leaving the center to decline and shift for itself.

High points for the reader of *Travels* are times when the author pauses to recapture a dialogue, complete with carefully limned descriptions of the persons talking, each nuanced and unique, bringing to life and coalescing the individuality, regionality, and universality of an incident or episode, its setting, and its participants. The rundown cabin he stayed at in Idaho among mountains "tufted with pines and deep-dusted with snow" (127-128) pales next to the supper he shared with the crusty proprietor and his restless son. They invited him to join them in the ramshackle but cozy back quarters for "baked ham, and beans, [and] ice cream" (130) served on "a square table covered with white, knife-scarred oilcloth" (132). For this traveler in quest of the genuine, it was a favor easy to accept, especially in a place specializing in "'Pies like mother would of made if mother could of cooked.'" Such vignettes authenticate the travels and make us feel like joining in.

ERIC NEWBY'S MOCK-EPIC TALE

- A Short Walk in the Hindu Kush -

Neither a short walk nor a trumped-up climb over a molehill, Newby's journey to Afghanistan to scale the 20,000-foot peak of Mir Samir makes little of much. *A Short Walk in the Hindu Kush*, published in 1958, and one of over two-dozen travel books written over his career, is primarily and tantalizingly a narrative of understatement. Not one to boast or employ hyperbole except for humorous effect, Newby chronicles in expanded diary mode the perils and obstacles to achieving a pipe dream.

Leaving his career in the fashion world, he pairs up with a veteran traveler and mountaineer, Hugh Carless. Together with a pack of paid guides and aids, they light out for the challenges of snowy peaks and vast glaciers. With considerable success, sharing an aptitude for languages and appreciating cultural differences, Newby and his partner, a former Indian Civil Servant proficient in Persian, strive to learn and speak the languages and dialects of those they encounter along the way. First, however, the duo rehearses for a few days in Wales under the guidance of an experienced climber. After becoming briefly acquainted with gear and procedures, their nascent pride in having advanced on the learning curve evaporates as they endure embarrassment by the superior performance of a couple of athletic young women. Admittedly, from the get-go, Newby (as his name might suggest) announces that he is a novice: "I had never been anywhere that a rope had been remotely necessary" (22).

Flying from London to Istanbul, from there boarding a ferry, after a debacle involving his wallet being stolen, Newby and his wife Wanda, who accompanies her husband for the first part of the trip, and Hugh take off on the road supposedly headed to Armenia. Having to backtrack because of not having read the map correctly, the party motors on to Persia and thence to Afghanistan. The delays on the road are magnified by a supposed hit-and-run incident. A good bit of the itinerary but not the most rigorous and exciting portions occurs after arriving at Kabul. The distance to northeastern Afghanistan's incredible heights slowly but laboriously shrinks.

Newby describes scrapes and bruises and harrowing, life-threatening incidents with telling detail and frequent bouts of humor, chiefly of the self-deprecatory stamp. The text is spiced with similes and metaphors that capture, epitomize, and intensify each step, trudge, and mile of the journey, each vertical inch (or meter) of ascent. When he receives word Hugh is game to accompany him, Newby notes, "Like an echo in a quarry his response came back" (23). Chapter 3, entitled "Birth of a Mountain Climber," mimics the first two chapter titles: "Life of a Salesman" and "Death of a Salesman." Emphasizing their starting point, undertaking trial spurts on hilly Welsh terrain practicing the ABCs of rappelling, he casually observes, "a flock of mountain sheep watched us go, making noises that sounded suspiciously like laughter" (31).

Bumps in the road are plentiful and include an incident in which they are arrested—the case being falsely but officially made and causing delay, humiliation, and misspent time in jail and in court—for running down a nomad whose lifeless body they had swerved to avoid hitting. Sickness, near starvation and dehydration, total exhaustion, and failed attempts to conquer certain planned peaks and passes complicate but do not stop the travelers or the fun and play of the language. In exasperation, undaunted, Newby comments, "Arguments" with officials over techniques and differences in points of view "shot backwards and forwards across the room like tennis balls" (54). Another time he employs hyperbole, comparing Russian stoves to "cannon . . . warming two rooms at once, needing whole forests of wood to keep them going" (56). When one of a fleet of numerous vehicles rented to complete segments of the journey peters out and Newby is cramped beneath it, a tool in one hand and a manual in the other, he complains, "It was like trying to read a first folio in a crowded train" (58). Newby ransacks academia, business, military history, and world and pop culture to embellish the telling, adroitly sashaying between documentary prose and figurative language. The book's title itself hints at the pervasive mock-epic point of view. That technique is used to downplay the serious implications in the string of hardships, accidents, and follies adumbrating the glorified diary of amateurs tramping in the footsteps and scaling the heights known only to the few fully qualified. These newbie mountaineers lurk in the shadows of those experts they strive to follow. Laughingly we witness Newby, in a Twain-like moment, pulling out an instructional pamphlet to gauge their progress and double-check on techniques when they clawed their way to an elevation just short of the summit.

Master of British understatement, Newby minimizes the dangers and defeats that befall them. Admittedly, early on, he confesses, "I was already afflicted with the gastric disorders that were to hang like a cloud over our adventure" (61). On this theme, and hardly his fault, the party faces culinary disasters and menus unfit for consumption, even while camping in the toolies and on foreign ground, ice, snow, and slush. One such unpalatable and indigestible incident is representative. "Normally an innocuous dish of curdled milk fit for the most squeamish stomach, it arrived stiff as old putty, the same colour and pungent" (64).

In travel, much is unpredictable. Snow and ice, dirt and sand and mud, rocky terrain, rivers, wind, and rain punctuate the itinerary. "In the morning we wake to find ourselves buried under twin mounds of sand" (65), he relates, adding that he had taken one sulphaguanidine pill each of the preceding sixteen hours. The solemn tone conjoined with verbal winks contributes to the disarming humor wrapping the story from beginning to end.

Natural phenomena and the outdoor struggle to endure and succeed against great odds are captured in the observation that "As we marched across the open space . . . the wind was hot like an electric hair dryer and strong enough to lean on" (66). A river they had to swim in widened to "a lake, shivering like a jelly between earth and sky." The branches lining the shore were "sharp as bayonets" (67). Dust blowing over the rough road as they drove resembled "a London fog"; it filled their mouths and reduced them to "mumble" (69). The hotel they stopped at furnished a breakfast consisting of "runny eggs and flies and dust all mixed inextricably together in an inedible mass" (70). Idling that afternoon in the heat, "Hugh was out completely, like a submarine charging its batteries" (70). Rest could hardly anesthetize them to withstand the "vast pot-holes," which the narrator judges to be "large enough to contain nests of machine-gunners," hinting at ghostly obstacles conspiring with natural impediments to their completing the big challenge for which they are traveling.

The narrative is filled with arduous and seemingly insurmountable obstacles handled with figurative fun that both enlarges and belittles the challenges faced and somehow overcome. Even the worst are dismissed with a humorous splash in the face. Bordering on burlesque, the mock-epic leans into caricature in some character sketches. The cook hired for the expedition is one such instance. Ghulam Naabi is described as "round and brown and fat and jolly and resembles a Christmas pudding. His eyes were like shiny currents and he was even done up in something that was like a white pudding cloth but was really an old white mess jacket" (82). The passage rivals Chaucer and Dickens combined, for it brings to mind the portraits of the cook on the pilgrimage to Canterbury and "the fat boy" in *Pickwick Papers*. Later on, the cook is seen devouring apricots and mulberries. "Like a mechanical shovel, Ghulam Naabi's hand rose and fell, scooping them from the basket and into his mouth until I thought he would burst. As the light failed, he seemed to grow larger like a white balloon" (104). The text is bejeweled and fraught with literally hundreds—often several on a single page—of felicitous similes that make its reading a joy and a marvel and collectively advance the mock-epic tone and treatment. Another of the meandering roads leading to the mountains stands out for its figurative, not simply literal, depiction: "The road wriggled on and on. It was like driving along the back of a boa-constrictor that had just enjoyed a good meal, and equally bumpy" (101). The distant snowless peaks resemble "dry . . . old bones" (100).

Not till a third or more of the way into the book, a fortnight having elapsed since their setting out, do we glimpse what lies ahead and serves as the chosen goal. "Now, ahead of us, the Hindu Kush mountains rose spiky and barren-looking out of the plain" (97). As they nudge into colder weather, lower temperatures, and higher elevations, they no longer sweat but shiver and are bothered and bitten by different breeds of insects. Authenticating the change, Newby writes, "My teeth were chattering like castanets" (116). Midway into the trip, Newby also discovers that his fashionably pointed-toe Italian boots had been acting up and that his feet were the worse for wear: "It was as if a tram had gone over them . . . and . . . my socks were full of blood. . . . My feet looked as though they had been flayed, as indeed they had" (117).

By then, makeshift encampments have taken a toll, and the party with all their gear and bundles of belongings strewn about "resembled ambushed settlers making a last stand" (119). Before nearing the icy plateau at the foot of the longed-for lofty peaks, they traverse a tiresome, hot, treeless valley, which "was like walking on red-hot corrugated iron" and where "The sun seemed to fill the entire sky like a great brass shield" (127). The immediate goal is to complete the trek, one of the many marathon days extending from before first light till dark, and reach a shady grove to recuperate and feed and water the horses. Another tedious valley they encounter is similarly bleak, the only plant life being "the limp and dying wild rhubarb that covered the lower slopes of the hill, like the flags of the losing side after a battle" (138). Fortunately, they soon approach the viewing distance of Mir Samir, which "seen from the west, was a triangle with a sheer face" (141). However, two slow-going days later, the perspective shifts, a familiar phenomenon experienced by inhabitants living at the base of a mountain summit or range. The higher mountain had become largely shuttered by a companion peak of 18,000 feet, part of a jagged ridge separated from the primary ridge by "a deep valley, the far side rising in a fiendish-looking unscalable ridge, serrated with sharp pinnacles, like a mouth full of filed teeth" (146). It seemed the right time to set up base camp and prepare for the ascent. Or would this prove to be a chimera?

As they commence the climb, they are tested on their readiness. "We moved up the glacier, plodding along with the unaccustomed crampons laced to our boots, clockwork figures, desiccated by the sun, our attention concentrated on the surface immediately ahead which we carefully probed with ice-axes for crevasses. . . . The light was very trying; even with goggles it was like driving into someone else's headlights. We were thirsty and all around us was running water. It was difficult to resist the temptation to scoop up a mouthful but the state of our insides was sufficient warning for us not to do so" (150). Contending as best they can with steeper incline and troublesomely deeper snow, they plod on.

Scaling the rock is difficult and takes a toll on the hands and the feet. Time is running out. They have to abort and retreat to their camp below, no less easy going down as going up. Regrouping, having caught a modicum of sleep before sunrise, the party tackles an adjacent glacier but has to give up again. Making it to 17,000 feet, they descend to 9,000. As they position themselves for a final attempt, the mountain view and prospect of reaching its summit overwhelm them. "We felt like dwarfs," Newby writes:

> On our right the whole southern aspect of Mir Samir revealed itself: the east ridge like a high garden wall topped with broken glass; the snow-covered summit; the glaciers receding far up under the base of the mountain in the summer heat; and below . . . wildernesses of rock pouring down to the first pasture, with the river running through it, a wide shallow steam fed by innumerable rivulets. To the east the mountains rose to a level 17,000 feet, then rising and falling like a great dipper, encircled the head of the valley, forming the final wall of the south-west glacier where we had made our unsuccessful effort among the ice toadstools on the other side only two days before. (167)

Onward, the party ventures. Encountering geological challenges, Newby reports, "we battled our way sweating and swearing horribly" (173). They congratulate themselves on reaching 18,000 feet, at which milestone, "Two thousand feet below us, like an enormous new frying-pan sizzling in the sun was the east glacier" (174). Their hopes are high, and they are exhilarated. They are determined to reach the summit in time to make it down and back to camp before total darkness while still capable of negotiating the return without succumbing to absolute exhaustion. Reality sets in, however, and, with no time to nurse regrets, they begin the descent to base camp to rest and retry the next day. Despite delays and obstacles, the party makes it up to 19,100 feet on the morrow. They persist a couple of hundred weary vertical feet farther, yet with only 700 feet remaining to the summit, they know it isn't humanly possible to obtain their goal and make it down in the dark to a safe level to camp. As it turns out, "the descent was terrible" (185). The wind and blizzard conditions slow their progress nearly to a crawl in their crampons, which they must repeatedly remove to scrape clear of ice. Darkness intensifying, contending with unbelievable fatigue, understandably somewhat crestfallen, and with bloody hands and sore feet, they ultimately make it down to a ledge where they indulge in nutrition, swallow sleeping pills, and drift off to well-earned slumber.

The rest of the book, rather anticlimactically, recounts the party's trek into adjoining Nuristan. Newby maintains momentum and keeps the reader's interest by delineating landscape features, commenting on local flora and fauna, describing persons they encountered and differentiating their apparel and habits, and interlarding pertinent bits of historical and cultural information. One conspicuous fact is that "Nuristan was a perfect hell of insect life" (229). In this part, though, Newby sounds less like an entomologist and more like an anthropologist. As is generally true in the travelogue genre, the last pages of the wrap-up look fondly to returning home. Such is the case with Newby, who, speaking in a decidedly valedictory voice, claims, "All of a sudden I felt that revulsion against an alien way of life that anyone who travels to remote places experiences from time to time. I longed for clean clothes; the company of people who meant what they said, and did it. I longed for a hot bath and a drink" (248). Present, too, is a note of happiness over having completed the mission, albeit settling unapologetically for a triumph a smidgen short of the tip. As Newby and his partner Hugh blow up their air mattresses on the eve of their departure, their last foreign host exclaims, "God, you must be a couple of pansies" (255). Hardly! The tale finishes fittingly on a note of mockery.

A Short Walk is an epic undertaking sketched in mocking rather than heroic tones. Deliberately in words subdued and, by contrast, at times with language intended to be over the top, Newby's prose is supple and poetic. The chosen point of view for the delivery clings to the pole or rocky ledge of the understated and avoids the opposite pole of boasting and soliciting congratulations. The heightening of the drama by such oblique strokes of the pen creates a more powerful result than achievable with mere reportage and fidelity to the stunning facts and details of the journey.

Pronounced with a straight face and counting on the reader's smile, Newby ensures that his chapter titles reinforce the mock-epic motif. They tend even to reflect on and play off one another. For example, the party's two ensuing struggles to conquer the intended summit are entitled "Round 1" and "Round 2"; the intervening chapter, in a casually allusive stroke, is captioned "Coming Round the Mountain"; the next chapter scores a win in the ring and is aptly titled "Knock-out." The sequence of attempts at victory is telegraphed in the chapter "Over the Top."

From the book's title to its chapter headings, from the first to the last page, by dint of the concerted play of language, the narrative skirts away from the heroic and epic and pursues a lighter, more comedic note. Newby gets maximum mileage for fuel expended with that technique, and we are accorded passage on an engaging epic journey onward and upward.

TRAVELS OF MARCO POLO

Unlike imaginary journey classics, Marco Polo's travelogue purports to be a true account. Granted, writers of fictional journey classics—Swift and Bunyan, for example—pretend that what they share is factual, but the truth of their works lies not in what actually happened but in their depiction of human nature. For twenty-six years in the late 13th Century, for commercial ventures on behalf of the Great Kublai Khan, Marco Polo, in company with his father and uncle, traveled from their native country of Italy to Persia, India, China, and other regions of the Near and Far East. His fascinating account of these journeys was done in collaboration with a writer named Rustichello, who was a fellow war prisoner in Genoa for a time. Much of what Polo observed and learned firsthand about the geography, culture, history, customs, and activities of the larger world was news to his contemporaries, whose purview was provincially European and decidedly Christian. Today the account of his travels likewise puts us in touch with the unknown, the marvelous, the exotic—with those parts of the world and those times in human history quite removed from us. The old trade routes and commercial traffic of the early Middle Ages, anticipating the explorations and discoveries of the Renaissance, come alive, and the reality of global competition and interdependence so familiar to us now is dawning in Polo's recollections.

The book is full of contrasts: Christians vs. infidels (the Saracens, the Jews, and the nearly ubiquitous "idolaters"), unparalleled wealth and luxury vs. penury and misery, hospitality vs. warfare, generosity vs. deprivation. It covers the ugly and the beautiful. It contains much that is shocking and incredible. It is chock full of information and details concerning different—*very* different—ways of life. Battles; marriage and sexual practices; food and drink preferences, including cannibalism; occupations and top-down social structures; various climate conditions; religious rites; particular punishments incurred for offenses, both heinous and seemingly trivial; burial customs; accumulation and exchange of jewels and spices; clothing habits as well as nudism; ship construction; data on significant rivers, mountains, flora and fauna, and other natural features; matters of architecture; gardening techniques—the work is encyclopedic. Overall, the tale has the spellbinding effect of romance. The narrative is replete with curious tidbits and exposition of civic achievements and cultural highlights. Among the wonders inventoried, Polo documents their early and extensive use of paper money, the painful but popular and prestigious practice of the wealthy to decorate their entire bodies with tattoos, and the institution of a mail delivery system antedating what in the American West became known as the pony express.

The details are stupendous. The Khan established a network of thousands of trusty horses and riders and enumerable, fully-furnished inns, stables, and livery stations (never more than forty miles apart) to spirit dispatches back and forth across his sprawling empire. The account is lavish with the inclusion and celebration of marvels. Stressing the authenticity and scope of his tale of travel, Marco Polo is set on giving the reader a straightforward report of the habits, rituals, and behavior of the Tartars.

The narrator takes pride in his intention of faithfully informing the reader of the wonders, geographical and cultural, he encounters upon leaving his homeland and venturing to a remote and largely unknown quadrant of the world. He delights in sharing the spectacular. The author takes the reader from extreme heat to extreme cold, apropos of climate differences. One place, Quilon, in India, is so scorching and the sun's heat so intense that it can barely be withstood. He contends that the rivers there can serve to boil an egg in under three minutes. The narrator's use of vivid details to drive home facts about climate is wonderfully evident in his description of Russia. He says the country is so cold that inhabitants can hardly tolerate it. But to adapt to the conditions, they ingeniously developed a system of heated huts to make it from point A to point B without freezing. Polo claims that he ran across men with bushy tails in the mountains in India. In several places, he spots unicorns. When he talks of stones that burn better than logs and emit heat but no flame, he may just be describing a form of coal rather than celebrating an utter novelty. But everywhere, he has his eye out for the unusual.

Polo's commanding personality and precocity come through with remarkable success in his absorbing narrative, loaded with claims of things never before witnessed. At the start (in the Prologue) and end (in the Epilogue), Polo rightfully extols his unique exploration and global legacy. He knew and celebrated that he was tilling new soil, covering new ground. He pioneered boldly, setting forth new and foreign records and discoveries for the amazement of those back home and an audience expanding to myriads of readers (armchair travelers) down through the ages. He informed his compatriots that the world and its regions of civilization were vaster and more advanced than reckoned, announcing wonders and oddities till then unthinkable, almost unimaginable, but in dreams and tales of fiction and wonder. Numerous explorations and tales by those who went on them have followed in Polo's wake. The world, at least that of his contemporary readers, was expanding, and Polo was definitely at the helm. His *Travels* would keep cartographers, professionals and amateurs alike, busy revising and charting new territories, even ahead of voyages in the offing that would necessitate further corrections to the evolving maps of the globe.

The travels are largely by sea and involve trekking across vast stretches of land by foot, horseback, and even caravans astride elephants and camels. As he travels from region to region, Polo registers what the chief local products are—from canes, shoes, ships, to silk, you name it. He identifies places that set records as both sources and volumes of consumers of commodities like sugar, ginger, and pepper. Why, in the city of Kinsai, in China, he exclaims, the pepper in the people's daily diet ratcheted up to 43 cart-loads weighing 223 pounds apiece! He appears to delight in impressing, at times shocking, the reader with staggering statistics and extraordinary practices. In one market, he comes across giant pears the size and weight of watermelons. Fine linen and rare gems frequently catch his admiring eye. Baghdad is particularly renowned for its concentrated wealth of precious stones and metals. In one provincial capital, he notes that all the men living there have gold enameled teeth. What people eat, how they dress, and what they do and believe are documented and illustrated as if from a traveler's diary and careful memory.

One aspect of storytelling is, of course, point of view. The rapport the narrator establishes and seeks to maintain with the reader, the dramatic framework as it were, is an integral part of a story, especially if the narrator is a traveler recounting a journey. Here the narrator, aiming to be the trusted guide, attempts to sort out and select what he thinks will be of interest to his readers, always the after-the-journey armchair passengers. Throughout, we get little phrases, variously translated, like "Let me tell you about it," "This is how it happened," or "Let us now change the subject." Sometimes he says there is nothing of interest in such a place, and he will skip onto something more entertaining or instructive. Other times, he says he will return to a subject when it is more appropriate. Occasionally, he will report that an event is not worth recording. He is very concerned that we believe him. In one case, he worries that if he told us the actual number of ships on a given river, we'd accuse him of lying. He nevertheless adds that in the instance related, the total number of vessels exceeds 15,000! A ploy to baffle and tease the astonished reader? Elsewhere he notes that he will skip over some of the marvels encountered because his readers would be incredulous, this caveat despite the many wonders he does choose to elaborate on in the book.

Writers and their readers mutually delight in the use of figurative language. It is interesting to note Marco Polo's use of litotes, hyperbole (though the exaggerations are frequently passed off as certainties), similes, catalogs, and motifs or formulae. Each writer develops a style. It is their signature. If you study it closely, you can copy another's distinctive signature or style. Most artists learn their trade and evolve their style by imitating and then adapting and, finally, discovering their technique—still with much borrowing. However, an added complication enters when we are dealing with a translation as we are here. Translations vary in completeness and readability and are not all based on the same manuscript fragments or the language of origin. Translators differ, sometimes notoriously, in faithfulness to the letter and spirit of the original, often wanting to put their own spin on it. Some editions of Marco Polo's *Travels* contain maps to help orient readers to the scale and locations of the itinerary. Most include an index, the more useful if annotated or with cross-references. All versions of the work are crammed with wonderful observations and present sweeping geographical and cultural reportage.

Travels of Marco Polo, whatever the translation, is a work guaranteed to satisfy a reader's wanderlust, for it gets the reader feeling sweaty and hungry, frightened and astonished, sated in things exotic and foreign. The customs and conventions of other civilizations and cultures, their ways, beliefs, and manners make a trip exhausting and refreshing.

SHIP AHOY

- Navigating *Gulliver's Travels* -

Gulliver's Travels, a prose work by Jonathan Swift (1667-1745), published in 1726, recounts the imaginary voyages of one Lemuel Gulliver. It is divided into four parts: Part 1, "A Voyage to Lilliput," where Gulliver figures as a giant among pygmies; Part 2, "A Voyage to Brobdingnag," which reverses the situation of Part 1, Gulliver this time parading as a Tom Thumb; Part 3, "A Voyage to Laputa, Balnibarbi, Luggnagg, Glubbdubdrib, and Japan," detailing the traveler's visits and interviews with kings and uppity-ups in which their customs and history are compared to those of Gulliver's compatriots and, as a highlight, his sojourn at the so-called Grand Academy of Lagado, at which educational institution experiments are conducted that rival science fiction; and Part 4, "A Voyage to the Country of the Houyhnhnms," the land of rational horses and detestable Yahoos. All told, a series of fascinating ports of call!

While the work purports to be a true and accurate account of the traveler's experiences, it is a blistering and amusing satire of how things are instead of how they could or should be. When one travels abroad, one naturally is given to comparing what is encountered with what goes on or passes for normal back home—both tale-teller and reader gain perspective by remarking on such differences. When Gulliver is small among the large, he and, by extension, the reader, who occupies the station of a silent but involved companion, have the opportunity to gauge the grossness of human activity. Vice versa, when Gulliver is super tall in a population of shorties, he and we have a splendid view of the pettiness of human nature. The lens is everything. The proportions and scale, twelve to one and one to twelve, help make a case for relativity, the vulnerability, and supposed or alleged superiority inherent in human institutions and nature. Gulliver is Swift's mouthpiece when he states, "Undoubtedly Philosophers are in the Right when they tell us, that nothing is great or little otherwise than by Comparison" (56). Swift's device of refocusing the lens of changing perspectives lends credence to his presentation of the abnormal and excessive. It is only when things are allowed to appear totally out of proportion, out of balance, that we are enabled to comprehend what is or should be normal or right—morally or even just physically. What is it that William Blake noted in his axioms from hell: "You never know what is enough unless you know what is more than enough?" The philosophy of excess is grounded in the classic conservative notion that moderation is what should be strived for and that it is best to pilot one's craft between extremes.

As in many travel narratives, the point of view from which the work is told is first-person. First-person helps us quickly identify with the traveler, the teller of the tales, whose surrogate traveler and beholder we become as we get engrossed in the events unfolding in the retelling. We turn into the "I." When we travel, for real or pretend, we can't help but compare where we are with where we have been and will be returning. That double focus adds power to our vision and is the basis for many insights gained from traveling. Prismatically, the past, present, and future merge into a complete vision, each aspect playing upon the others, magnifying our total vision of life and intensifying our insight.

Swift is having and presenting fun while simultaneously being (and inviting the reader to be) serious. We share the ironic pose with the author and appreciate Gulliver's straight-faced recitation (whose name is a play on "gullible"). In the careful documentation of latitude and longitude details, the names of the ships and their captains, references to navigational paraphernalia, and the scrupulous recording of measurements and empirical minutiae, Gulliver comes off as a stickler for accuracy. In Swift's hands, Gulliver is not simply a surgeon and an absentee husband and father indulging his wanderlust by embarking on long voyages to foreign lands but the amateur natural philosopher intent upon recording the truth. Gulliver's penchant for telling it the way it was assists Swift in goading the reader to accept the incredible as credible. But, as readers and after-the-fact fellow travelers, we refuse to swallow everything Lemuel Gulliver presents as entirely plausible or factually indisputable. The satire depends on our perception of how Swift intends us to view the circumstances Gulliver recounts, on what we discern Swift's take on them as the creator behind the make-believe. Humor arises from the discrepancy between Gulliver's reception of what happened to him and what we in league with the author believe to be desirable or reasonable. We are swept along into the incredible by the presentation of it by the observer as factual. The narrator's vision is not that of the author or reader, who together maintain critical judgment about the things the narrator is prone to rave over or deplore, his background and prejudices coloring his observations and conclusions. Swift uses satire to get at abuses in learning, religion, politics, language, the professions, and society, with pride, the chief of the seven deadly sins, underlying the list of encyclopedic shortcomings characterizing human beings.

The letter from Captain Gulliver to his cousin appended to the work, and the note from the Publisher to the Reader, is part of the game Swift is playing. It is a pitch for authenticity. Swift mimics the highfalutin treatises of his day's scientists, researchers, and explorers. His recorder fits the mold. The Royal Society lurks in the shadows of the seemingly enlightened and resourceful Gulliver. The reader of *Gulliver's Travels* derives pleasure from penetrating the mold and acquiescing with the author that while there are better ways to conduct human affairs, those ways are hardly of the order that Lemuel subscribes to. Nor are they within the pale of what humankind is likely to strive toward or adopt.

Moreover, while Swift is not arguing that humankind must settle for what is ignoble, he insists that humankind will not achieve perfection. Swift believed in humans' frailty and the need for their salvation. For Swift, a man of the cloth and Dean of St. Patrick's Cathedral, men and women were fallen creatures in need of redemption. Any notion that humans were advancing as a species, he denied. *Gulliver's Travels* is a testament to Swift's outlook on the potential of human beings to err.

It is interesting and entertaining to contemplate the difficulties Gulliver experiences in transitioning back to his normal world after each voyage, particularly the troubled adjustment he faces upon returning from his last journey. Given his brainwashing while living with the

Houyhnhnms and enjoying their enlightened company, small wonder that when he returns to his own lot, he feels more at home in the stable with the horses than in his house with his family. Like all travelers, upon returning home and to things familiar but seemingly remote due to the spell of absence, he experiences cultural shock and adjustment. He has spent time in foreign places and become acquainted and comfortable with customs that differed radically from those he had intimately known and taken for granted in his native country. But is it simply a case of traveler's syndrome? The extreme change in Gulliver's perspective is symptomatic of the traveler's espousal of the ways and attitudes of those with whom he has been visiting. Here, the when-in-Rome factor is the horses, the quadrupeds he saw as superior in reason to the Yahoos. He dismisses the Yahoos as ill-mannered two-legged creatures resembling his own species in physical appearance. Characteristically, a traveler returns changed, more aware of immediate circumstances because of having sojourned elsewhere, where customs and scenery are novel. It takes a while to get back to what one was used to, debrief, and process the return. Whether Gulliver has succumbed to the deadly sin of pride or been infected with a case of misanthropy, the reader will have to judge.

From both the author's and the reader's perspective, Gulliver has not been improved by his erstwhile life among livestock and has little substance on which to base his superiority to his countrymen, family, and neighbors, whose company he cannot now abide. We realize, as Gulliver does not, that their fallibility does not equate to that of the Yahoos and that the seeming perfection of the Houyhnhnms doesn't square with the nature of the animals in Gulliver's barn. It is doubtful that they could thread needles or rear their young in the fashion that prevailed in the land of the Houyhnhnms. Nor is it likely that the family and townspeople to whom Gulliver returns share the odor and off-putting antics of the Yahoos. His pride in mastering the gait and nasalized utterances of the horses he admires for their reliance on reason is misplaced and laughable. So too are his revulsion at seeing the reflection of his own two-legged body and his being taken aback by the Yahoo resemblance he encounters in the society of humans. Officially rejected from the company of the Houyhnhnms as an anomaly too close to a Yahoo in looks and behavior, Gulliver regrets that he must return to his homeland.

Swift didn't subscribe to the view that humans are rational animals and a species demonstrating moral progress. Instead, he defined humans not as rational creatures but as creatures *capable* of reason but subject to passions. Try as they may, he argued, humans by nature cannot fully control their desires. Theologically, Swift viewed humans as fallen creatures, endowed with passions and reason, which mix accounted for their struggle, often in vain, to achieve decency and accord with one another. The visit to faraway lands to study other attitudes and ways of doing things puts into perspective, by contrast, the history of civilization as Gulliver recounts it for his foreign audiences. The places Gulliver travels to are not utopias or mere fantasies so much as lenses through which the readers of his travels may view Western civilization's shortcomings and qualified triumphs. Ultimately, *Gulliver's Travels* pinpoints where humans fit on the scale of things and beings, from the earthly to the heavenly.

Over the course of his journeys, Gulliver undergoes a transformation. He sets out as a strident defender of civilized Europeans, one who shares their habits, outlook, mannerisms, and beliefs but is admittedly aware of instances of perversion and evil. Upon scrutiny and by visiting and living among societies either seemingly exempt from the particular prejudices, vices, and failings of his compatriots or, as his acquaintance expands, subject to different versions of moral weakness, he increasingly detaches himself from his origins. He gradually and ultimately accedes to the outlook and mores of the Houyhnhnms, with whom he resided for half a decade. His travels culminate in an acute antipathy for his own race, denouncing them as loathsome irrational creatures.

Satire is a powerful tool to deflate pride. The travelogue genre, which Swift is parodying, is a splendidly innocuous means of exposing the faults and fabric represented by the traveler and his ilk. To critique a civilization directly might well lose the critic a good share of the audience. Humor and imagination coupled with corrective insight, which accounts for the impact of satire, achieve what sermons and treatises cannot. Satire succeeds where they might offend. The serious or tendentious may turn off souls who otherwise would willingly connect through the mechanism of comic distance. The mileage that Swift gains from poking fun at travel literature contributes to the success of the satire. The work is at the same time a precursor to the novel, a children's classic, a piece of fantasy and science fiction, and a full-scale satire—all in the guise of a travelogue.

The reader is brought into the far-fetched via the familiar all along the way. Swift's comparisons evoke the real world, the England and Ireland of his day, and vividly portray one after the other of the exotic lands he explores. All is described in proportion to the dimensions and conditions peculiar to the country he is visiting. In Lilliput, Gulliver the giant assists the tiny five-inch-plus high inhabitants trying in vain to put out a fire in the palace with a brigade of "Buckets . . . about the Size of a large Thimble" (31). He extinguishes the flames in minutes by urinating on them in the moonlight. His heroic action backfires, however, when later it causes his eviction from Lilliput, where the law forbids "any Person . . . to make water within the Precincts of the Palace" (31). The vessel he builds to sail away from Lilliput consumes "the Tallow of three hundred Cows for [its] greasing" (48), a quantity underscoring the relative sizes of things and creatures in the realm of England versus in the country of Lilliput.

In Brobdingnag, Gulliver remarks, "The Sound of his Voice," that of a giant like all the residents there, "pierced my Ears like that of a Water-Mill" (58). The farmer's daughter, who cares for the belittled Gulliver as though he were her pet, "put me on her own Bed, and covered me with a clean white Handkerchief, but larger and coarser than the Main Sail of a Man of War" (61). Little Lemuel contends with enormous wasps, "humming louder than the Drones of as many Bagpipes" and "as large as Partridges" (75). The naturalist in Gulliver prompts him to collect specimens whenever and wherever possible, provided they are portable. In the instance of the attack by insects, he extracts their stingers as souvenirs, reporting that he "found them an Inch and a half long, and as sharp as Needles. I carefully preserved them all, and having since shewn them with some other Curiosities in several parts of *Europe*, upon my return to *England* I gave three of them to *Gresham College* [the meeting place of the Royal Society, a fact Swift's contemporary readers would not need footnoted], and kept the fourth for my self" (75). The spoof goes deeper. Gulliver, as an illustrious representative of civilized mankind, a linguistically savvy and well-mannered, modest gentleman, is not only reduced in stature but is bruised by hailstones, carried off once by a dog and later by a bird, stumbles into a mole-hole, and jumping short of the mark falls into a cow pie—not a pretty picture of a grand man of culture. Gulliver nevertheless perseveres in his belief in the nobility of humanity till he finally reverses his esteem and, with the faulty vision of pride, excepting himself but condemning the rest of the human race, succumbs to a case of impaired vision tantamount to misanthropy. At the book's close, however, Gulliver progresses in getting used to the company of other humans, starting with his wife and family. It is hard to remain sober when reading about the cultural shocks that Gulliver experiences upon returning from his voyages to far-flung lands over some sixteen years. Motivated by a thirst to see the wide world, "my insatiable Desire of seeing foreign Countries" (50), Gulliver adventures into locations where he is inevitably positioned to redefine human potential and achievement. He surrenders his admiration for his compatriots and sheds his initially hard-held optimism. However, by dint of the irony the work possesses, Swift causes the reader to qualify, not entirely share, Gulliver's increasing disenchantment. As an absorbing travel tale, the journey is finally a discovery of the heights and depths to which human nature is destined. In the company of Gulliver, we witness both the grossness and the pettiness of human behavior and the ongoing difficulty of balancing reason and passion.

FOOTPRINTS IN THE SAND

- Robyn Davidson Crossing the Australian Desert -

Published in 1980, Robyn Davidson's *Tracks* chronicles a young woman's marathon trek of nearly two thousand miles across the Lower Continent. Partly astride a camel but much of the time exhaustingly on foot and alone, she perseveres. Occasionally, particularly when accompanied by Aboriginal guides, her routine is varied. Also, at strategic points, she meets up with a young photographer from *National Geographic*, the sponsor to whom she reluctantly yields a portion of her coveted independence in exchange for needed financial assistance. She immediately earns publicity and is tattooed "the camel lady" (142). For her this is the trip of a lifetime.

The travel tale moves forward with appealing figurative language, authenticating detail, and penetrating psychological realism. There is no need to suspend disbelief; the trip is so well prepared for and the text is so plausibly narrated. Before setting off on a camel caravan across seemingly endless miles of desert, Robyn spends three-fourths of a year acquainting and training herself with the animals, their peculiarities, abilities, and limitations. She gets deft at making, adjusting, putting on, and taking off saddles, gear packs, and harnesses. But she postpones the trip for a year until she can earn enough to purchase her own pack animals and supplies. Meanwhile, she does not shirk the hard work and preparation that such an ambitious journey entails—learning leather crafts that will pay off later on during the trip and gaining experience in dealing with the quirks and ailments of the animals. She temporarily works and lives in a pub to survive and build up her reserves.

Following a hundred pages of preparation, the author undertakes a dry run to get the kinks out before starting the epic journey. It turns out to be eight days in hell, "not easily forgettable" (89). The author pictured the individuals in her group as so many "plucked chickens" (86). It serves as a preview, but because it is neither extended nor solo, it hardly represents the itinerary looming ahead. Daunting challenges ahead of her include becoming capable of keeping her bearings on a largely unmarked route, withstanding hardships of weather and terrain, negotiating an ever-formidable surface of shifting sands and hostile plants, and fending off wild bull camels on the rampage.

When off for real, she has to be her own veterinarian, called on to nurse her camels when they are afflicted by injury or sickness, ever vigilant in looking out for food and water to sustain them and seeing to it that they are bedded down and securely tethered at nightfall and when pausing for rest. Otherwise, they would, and do, head back or wander off in a different direction when there is a chance. The heat and wind of the day and the cold of the night translate to sweat, chills, thirst, and exhaustion. At times, she is so fatigued and beset by the challenges that she suffers hallucinating moments and yields to interior debates over the worth of persisting with her solitary mission of a nearly sea-to-sea trek. Though resolute, she almost daily succumbs to doubt, acknowledging that the scheme appears to be turning out to be more a nightmare than a dream. But she manages to yank herself back from chronic bouts of defeat, some painfully extended, to a renewed aura of confidence. While in ebullient moods, "my aloneness was a treasure I guarded like a jewel" (41). When overcome by the prospect of failure, she yearns for the companionship of an Aboriginal guide or one of the friends she had bid farewell to upon embarking on her lonely journey. While she loathes the prospect of sharing time with a media person, fearing that such a presence would threaten to sensationalize or depersonalize the venture of her lifetime, she concedes that some privacy and independence will have to be surrendered to succeed with her plans. The National Geographic's subsidy and accompanying offer to publish her diary (with illustrations and fanfare) is both a dilemma and a necessary evil.

In the end, what helps make the tale convincing and empathetic for the reader is the ebb and flow of emotion experienced by the narrator and captured and conveyed with stunning verisimilitude. The story culminates in a victory somewhat bittersweet. Not romanticized, the tale is one of personal fulfillment earned by the sweat of the brow and turmoil of the traveler's soul. One could call it a coming of age, for it records a youth triumphing over the vicissitudes borne of a dream translated into reality. *Tracks* fits the genre of a pilgrimage, sharing the trajectory of temptation and trial en route to a seemingly celestial destination, the reward for faithfully staying on and not permanently straying from the path forward.

The text is enlivened by humor and figurative language, balancing the literal and the metaphorical. The style of the narrative, at times, becomes hyperbolic. In detailing her nervous apprehension, she exaggerates, suggesting that she has been "chewing my nails up to the elbow" (82). The sensation of "standing near" her erstwhile camel boss, whose "grin disappeared like greasy water down a plug-hole," is, she suggests, "like being close to a fallen power line—all dangerous, crackling energy" (12). In pinpointing alliteration, she describes the convicts that originally landed in Australia as "biased, bigoted, boring, and, above all, brutal" (19). Her trip, however, teaches her the worth of the Aboriginals, a few of whom join her singly to guide her through especially treacherous segments. Eddie, a diminutive Aboriginal with more gesture than voice—her facility in their language still somewhat halting even at the end—becomes a genuine friend and is admired for his seemingly intuitive knowledge of the intricate desert environment. The traveler learns firsthand the sorry plight of the Aboriginals relocated to reservations, a situation paralleling and reminiscent of how native American nations were consigned to reservations typically located in the undesirable wasteland.

The mode of travel in this tale is distinctive. The account provides information and an on-the-move illustration of the nature of camels, starting with the author's initial bonding with the eight camels in Kurly Ranch, where she worked for several months as an apprentice. The desert beasts of burden brought to the lower continent years earlier and allowed to expand in wild herds and roaming packs are treated by Davidson as if they are children, her children. Sometimes—each bearing a separate name and personality—they are coddled, cared for, and spoken to as family members. Caught by their mistress in the act of running away, the camels "hung around me like flies, shuffling their feet, looking embarrassingly at the ground, or coyly through their elegant lashes, acting apologetic and loving and remorseful" (82). They are consistently depicted anthropomorphically. Regarded as "home-bodies" (82), they are seen as creatures capable of embarrassment and trickery. Her entourage includes a dear dog, Diggety, a sleeping bag partner and constant companion and confidant. When he dies from poison shortly before the journey's end, the tale turns elegiac, and the tragic loss gnaws away at both the purpose of life and the ultimate feast of victory.

The narrator of this tale of travel, in a convincing blend, teeters between exacerbation and satisfaction, self-elation and self-abnegation. At times, the narration pauses while the traveler assesses and dramatizes her state of being, often a blur of bifurcated interior, solipsistic individualism (both desired and deplored), and social acceptance and relief. She is guarding her trip as hers alone. While fighting to keep Rick, the photographer from National Geographic, from becoming a partner or colleague, she surrenders to him in a sleeping bag. She ultimately accepts his status as a friend, even while he intervenes at points to take copious pictures of what she continues to claim as a private domain.

Part Two of *Tracks*, entitled "Shedding Burdens," says a lot about how much we take on our journey. Throughout, Davidson delineates the nuances of desert life, including its peculiar sounds and silences, recorded respectively by the solitary traveler and by the caravan and family of animals—a dog, a toddler camel, and three adult camels, one a female (mother of the toddler) and the other a pair of bulls. She attempts to travel light, jettisoning items that prove to be too burdensome, including articles of clothing. Indeed, as the trip wears on, she habitually prefers to travel naked, letting the sweat and dust cake on her flesh and simulating an animal's natural outfitting against all weathers and obstacles.

The title of the travel book refers to the all too frequently ill-defined trail being followed, tantamount to the myriad and constant challenges besetting a pathfinder. A wrong decision can result in lost mileage that must be made up. The epic character of the tale is evident in the obscurity and difficulty of the route traveled. Also epic are the catalogs describing birds, plants, and creatures that predominate.

The tale is a pilgrimage, with the daily pace set at twenty miles, Sunday honored as a day of rest, and an anticipated completion calendar of six to eight months. This pilgrim's progress is marked by much introspection, given its primarily solitary nature, but simultaneously it serves as a primarily peaceable kingdom on the march. With compassion reminiscent of Francis of Assisi, the narrator cares for and befriends her band of animals. In a series of threatening encounters, she has to vanquish a foe or two to keep her own company intact and continue the journey. Aside from a rare expression of anger, even to the point of unnecessary cruelty and not simply self-defense, instances abound of her kinship with the animals. When on the third day out, she discovers a road that was not on the map, she panics: "My little heart felt like a Macaw in a canary cage" (118). In one of her numerous observations regarding her loneliness, she tells herself, "Do not flap around like a winged pigeon" (118). She commiserates with her "poor dumb entourage" (119). It is almost as though she is one of the pack animals, but she is ever the leader, and they are reined in as followers, regardless of the leeway they are permitted when forward progress is not in jeopardy.

The varied scenery and habitat are painted with verbal brushstrokes befitting the teller of a tale of travel. The immensity of the continent is made manifest by the dwarfing perspective given of the meager yet stately troop crossing the desert largely unassisted and as a rite of initiation. *Tracks* takes its place among chosen volumes of tales of travel worthy of being followed by the ambitious armchair traveler searching for a novel and rewarding trek, one that simultaneously celebrates geography and selfhood. The book is also the stuff of which a movie was made.

Davidson's affinity for the desert as a place to be, study, and meet the challenges of traversing is echoed in her second volume, *Desert Places*, set in India a decade after the trip narrated in *Tracks*. It is hardly a sequel, however. Accompanied by nomads and myriads of sheep and goats, Davidson endured contaminated water, a meager diet, fatigue, and disease in a region and culture, the Rabari of northwestern India, fast fading into oblivion and being usurped by modern times. An outsider for the year's journey, she surrenders her privacy and has to lump linguistic ignorance and entirely foreign ways. A combination of the will and the mercenary motivates the traveler and keeps her going to the bitter finish. Accordingly, the second account rings somewhat false in motive and falls short in the integrity of achievement. Maybe it is simply a case of the firstborn being begotten with greater gusto. The truth of her assertion that "the desert is no place for a dilettante" (112) becomes abundantly clear as her maiden tale of travel, *Tracks*, unwinds.

MARK TWAIN ABROAD

Published in 1870 and based on a group excursion to Europe and the Middle East two years earlier, *The Innocents Abroad* assured Twain's international stature as a writer. Going as a newspaper correspondent, Twain had his travel expenses paid. The resultant travel book was an immediate success, well documented, narrated with wit, verve, and a sharp focus. The fact that he did not go alone or accompanied by just one fellow traveler but by a boatload of passengers, sixty-five altogether, serves as the platform for defining a latter-day pilgrimage, both secular and sacred in its impulses. Many participants were far more conservative than Twain, though a few shared his rebellious enthusiasm and overwhelming curiosity to explore and carry out escapades ashore. These sorties get the small adventurous party into centers of ancient civilizations and, often to their surprise, into the throes of racial and religious commotion.

From the beginning, Twain is optimistic about opportunities to see a big part of the world, meet the whole array of classes, and observe from close vantage sights pulsating with history and drama and undergoing vast change. As he put it, "I travel to learn" (xvii,159). He is an eager student intent on recording it all and imparting the knowledge and insights he gains to his readers. He indulges in round-the-clock activity on and off the ship, never passing up a chance to get a firsthand grip on scheduled ports and expeditions. The itinerary left a lot up to the choice and interest of members of the excursion. Some are content to cling to the ship when optional tours are available. Not Twain. He acknowledges that he, a dedicated traveler, is going to remote places expressly to share his experience later with those back home. The pace is fast. Making up a word, he notes as they steam into the Mediterranean, "We are getting foreignized rapidly, and with facility" (xi,98). At the end of the journey, he speaks for all travelers when he exclaims the truth that "Travel is fatal to prejudice, bigotry, and narrow-mindedness" (650)—at least, that is its potential and best result.

The pilgrims visit a galaxy of sacred and secular sites: countless cathedrals, castles, palaces, and museums. In France, Twain visits the gardens at Versailles, Notre Dame cathedral, and other Parisian landmarks, witnesses the Cancan in action at night, and sees the treasures of the Louvre during the day. In Italy, he takes in Genoa, Venice and St. Mark's Square, the Grand Canal and its distinctive gondolas, and the past preserved in Pompeii by the eruption of Mount Vesuvius. The gothic cathedral in Milan he praises as "a forest of graceful needles" and "a poem wrought in marble" (xviii,171 & 172). Other de rigueur stops were the Coliseum and miscellaneous other famous ruins of Rome and the Duomo and the Uffizi Gallery in Florence. In Athens, "just as the earliest tinges of the dawn flushed the eastern sky and turned the pillared Parthenon to a broken harp hung in the pearly horizon" (xxxii,351), the group toured the ruins of the Acropolis. Places varied and storied like the great pyramids and the Sphinx in Egypt, a Bedouin encampment and a verdant oasis, and numerous sites in Palestine associated with the life of Jesus and the early Christian church rounded out the sightseeing. Besides offering traces of both the Old and New Testaments, Jerusalem was remembered by Twain for its crooked stony streets so narrow, he guesses, that "cats could have jumped double the distance without extraordinary exertion" (liii,559). Galilee, Ephesus, and venerable Damascus completed the Holy Land tour. Disappointedly, however, as Twain laments, many formerly thriving villages of significance in history had morphed into nothing more than dumps in the desert and rock-laden hills.

Innocents Abroad is an extensive survey. *A Tramp Abroad*, appearing a decade later, does not aim to sweep across the landscape and entire waterfront. The former is pitched for a beginner and avid reconnoiterer; the latter suits a seasoned reader and explorer looking for out-of-the-way places. *Innocents* is a lively factual account brimming with geographical and historical detail. *A Tramp* is largely a tour de force, rivaling other imaginary journeys in which verisimilitude is offset by exaggeration, humor, wit, satire, and emphasis on farfetched adventure. Humor in

Innocents is more droll, less raucous and Rabelaisian. Its interpolated legends, fewer and more germane, are ancillary to the itinerary and focus of the trip. In contrast, the interlarded stories, legends, and lengthy tales that occupy much of the space in *A Tramp* are often digressions. Preempting the emphasis on travel per se, they become the focus. *A Tramp* incorporates standard sightseeing fare and elaborate artifice at tale-telling—two broad avenues pursued in travel literature. *Innocents* is a travelogue, a work consistently centered on sightseeing and reckoning the importance, scale, history, and impact of places, persons, and customs encountered en route. The chosen modes of travel in *Innocents* reflect and expedite the narrator's lust for lingering at each step of the projected itinerary. Ever present is the phenomenon of a journey and a traveler informing the reader based on observations made and recorded in a diary, expanded by reference to other authorities and embellished with humor and opinions. All are presented in a style crafted to put matters into high relief. Carefully chiseled strokes reveal details and nuances, sometimes magnifying the subtleties and often exposing the reality—always the truth—rather than perpetuating myths or conceptions unsubstantiated by actual observation and critical assessment. The narrator calls on collateral authorities, outside the guides and guidebooks repeatedly lampooned, to throw scenes into greater relief. Legends, newspaper accounts, passages from literature and travel books, references to the Bible and to religious and cultural idiosyncrasies, and charts and lists enlarge the scope and illumine the picture of the journey. The narrator's perspective is an essential element in the genre. The appeal of tales of travel arises from the fact that they are not, as guidebooks are, confined to the mere recitation of information. The double role of the narrator of the trip is to be a filter and a reliable, engaging guide.

Innocents Abroad is very different from the travel book that followed. While incorporating Twain's penchant for humor, especially by way of exaggeration, *Innocents* coheres around the theme of travel in Europe and the Middle East. It is packed with historical, religious, and ethnic backgrounds. Moreover, because on the initial journey, Twain is part of a group, we get not only his and his friends' escapades but also interesting observations and incidents involving the other participants. The itinerary is indispensable to the book's success. Not so in *A Tramp Abroad*, where the preposterous and the incredible and the humor sprung from them are their own reason for being. Travel to and presence in other lands serve as jumping-off points to engage the narrative voice in legends and tales, the more bizarre and far-fetched the better. In *Innocents*, readers become more knowledgeable for having accompanied the author on the pilgrimage. They are refreshed and amused by the novelties involving the narrator and persons and places encountered, as well as by the history and lore.

In *Innocents*, the traveler-narrator stays on course. Directly following the preliminary presentation of the nature and scope of the journey at hand and the itinerary reported in the newspaper announcement, Twain boards the ship and addresses personal and immediate matters concerning the embarkation, weather, and make-up and attitude of those aboard. Stormy weather delays the departure, but as the ship heads out, he takes toll of the crew and passengers. Glorying in his sea legs the first morning on the billowy sea, he comments on the condition of the others, many of whom, much older than he, are sorely affected by the turbulence of the water and bobbing of the ship. In succession, all end their brief salutations with "*Oh*, my!" (iii,33-34) as they hasten off to relieve themselves. Next, in colorful language, Twain introduces the five resident captains. Then follows a description of the passengers and their activities. Everybody intends to keep a journal; all begin, but all soon quit, including a millionaire's son whose father told him he must maintain a diary. In the course of the voyage and the many stops along the way, Twain returns to the ship's passengers and crew as subjects to draw contrasts between Americans and the foreigners they're meeting. He mingles chiefly with others prone to play cards and who share his pleasure in smoke and drink, crave adventure, and want to maximize opportunities for gaining first-hand knowledge of the lands visited on this once-in-a-lifetime excursion.

The first chance for the wayfarers to observe and indulge comes when the ship arrives at the Azores, islands inhabited by ignorant, poor, and unclean but happy farmers. They plod along with their donkeys, planting corn that will be ground into meal when ripe. However, the wonderful thing about the Azores is the quality of their roads. Twain observes how vastly superior their road system is to that back home in America. As the voyage advances beyond the Straits of Gibraltar and exotic Tangier and onward to dock at and travel inland from ports along the Mediterranean, landmarks are systematically identified and extensively explored, even when off-limits. Twain, an adventurous doctor friend, and another rebellious chap he hangs out with, habitually disregarding quarantines and other dangers, surreptitiously abandon the anchored ship, often in the relative safety and complexity of darkness, to explore. Their escapades punctuate the more staid excursions on the prescribed itinerary and keep the reader amused and intimately involved, not passively following the order of the day on or off the ship. Especially given that Twain deliberately takes advantage of all options for side trips afforded by the unique design and appeal of "the great Pleasure Excursion to Europe and the Holy Land" (I,19). Like Chaucer, Twain joins a band of pilgrims, not at the Tabard Inn and not on a horseback ride to Canterbury but aboard a steamship, *Quaker City,* headed for Jerusalem and adjacent shrines and sites of Europe and the Middle East. Subtitled "The New Pilgrims' Progress," *Innocents Abroad* is not the setting forth for the celestial city by Bunyan's solitary Christian. More like the pilgrims in *The Canterbury Tales*, Twain and his fellow innocents keep one eye on the shrine of the destination and the other eye intent on enjoying secular matters.

Twain's account of his travels in *Innocents* is thorough. His intimate knowledge of the Scriptures started when he attended Sunday school and church. His voluminous reading of guidebooks, history, and literature, ancient and modern, shows up and gives his writing depth. At the same time, he mediates between myth and fact, yielding the reader insight into the vagaries and extremities of civilizations past and present. He satirizes Romans and Christians for their barbarous ways, juxtaposing events involving gladiators in the Coliseum and tortures committed during the Inquisition. He is taken aback by the superstition and gullibility over relics and legends that people have succumbed to at the church's direction for its profit and hegemony. He is candid about the sham behind the inestimable board feet that invariably, in grotto after grotto, are pronounced genuine splinters and hunks of the cross on which Christ was crucified. And he scoffs at the trumped-up multitude of exhumed bones of saints on display. The book is an expose of the untruths of the past and a setting forth of what was and what endures. Twain erases the indelible and romanticized impressions that many have of the Holy Land. As he documents, numerous sites have become cluttered with signs and souvenirs. A plethora of venerated places are shown not to be flowing with milk and honey, if they ever had been, but are wastelands of parched deserts and ruins. He fills in the blanks and sets the record straight with background information and firsthand descriptions of the shambles of edifices of former architectural splendor. Twain is an iconoclast. He exposes folly and admits to being sick and tired of the fulsome praise he hears or reads of the old masters and the distorted claims of guides and guidebooks. He prides himself on telling honestly what he saw and discovered and what his readers would see and experience were they to travel where he traveled. His purpose is to tell the truth and dispel myths.

Published in 1880, a decade after *Innocents Abroad*, *A Tramp Abroad* covers some of the same ground previously traversed, though not entirely on foot as the book's title implies. Not a sequel and hardly a straightforward travel book if there is such a thing by Twain or any other writer. *A Tramp Abroad* is a collection of sundry tales, legends, sketches (some pictorial, others verbal, but tied together), spoofs, and sightseeing commentary. The narrator pursues a leisurely pace and affords himself desultory privileges, opening up to humor almost everywhere.

In *A Tramp*, Italy and other countries in Europe get short shrift. France and the German-speaking countries are the main focus. The scope of the itinerary of *A Tramp* is not as extensive as *Innocents*, the maiden voyage, which logged a total of 20,000 miles at sea and on land. Walking limits distances, but the book's preoccupation with amusement and storytelling is a more influential factor impelling the tour and determining its direction.

The tall tales, exaggerations, self-deprecations, and mock self-congratulations that the book is replete with, elicit humor. The ostensible double purpose of the trip is to study the seemingly incomprehensible German language and to advance in the knowledge and criticism of art—both ambitions treated with hilarity and satire. Twain and his sidekick visit an array of prominent and remote places in Europe, starting with Germany, where they hope to learn to speak, read, and write German. There and continuing on the Continent, they are intent on appreciating the masterpieces on show in world-famous galleries. Twain even hopes to be inspired to try his hand at drawing and painting. The journey gets off with a bang at Heidelberg Castle as the author and his partner attend the ceremony of illumination and fireworks. A chunk of time in the old university city is spent observing daily duels fought by students comprising the five vying fraternities, each corps with its distinctively colored caps and out to gain victory and scars to enhance its reputation for bravery.

The book's humor manifests in a panoply of hilarious and witty ways. The text offers numerous instances of zeugma and wordplay ranging from puns and malapropisms to linguistic twists and specimens of convoluted orthography, etymology, and pronunciation. At points in the text, a foreign word, such as the simple German word *wo* for the English *where*, mocks the pedantic affectation of parading Latin or French phrases and offers comic evidence that progress is being made by the travelers in their avowed quest to become learned and more worldly wise.

In *A Tramp* as in *Innocents*, both intent upon capturing aspects of European travel, Twain caricatures Americans and pokes fun at the ways of the foreigners whom they visit. Guides and guidebooks are put in the stocks as if they were to be laughed at by the often gullible public and punished by one who knows or learns better and exposes the guide's folly and constant pretense to erudition. The two books vary in the modes of travel employed, and the form of travel taken is a subject of comment and interest.

A Tramp Abroad is more than a tale of travel; it is a collection of stories of a traveler. In the narrator's hands, the itinerary serves as a clothesline for hanging out digressions and stories and legends, most laced with humor and characteristically outrageous, and all wrung from the spots visited and the persons and incidents encountered en route. Also, Twain's sketches, drawn freehand and deliberately consisting of oddities, and his remarks on them contribute to the book's humor and help argue for the authenticity of his trip. They handily serve as evidence and exhibits of his having visited all such persons and places and proof of having engaged in the wild and far-fetched events he reports. Among the sketches of monuments is a silhouette of a leaning tower, part of an old German fortification, which they saw and climbed. Complementing his sketch of a horse-drawn carriage they rode in is the amateur artist's mock-criticism of its shortcomings. As his own art critic, Twain observes that "the wagon is not traveling as fast as the horse is," that the perspective is out of whack, and that the figure of a man trying to get out of the way is too small. Still, despite its flaws, the poker-faced narrator notes, the sketch "was exhibited in the Paris Salon of 1879," where regrettably, because it was only a "study," he scoffs, it did not win a prize (xiv,54).

The title itself, *A Tramp Abroad*, teases, hinting at a vagabond or low-class character on the road and on another level suggesting an encapsulated walking tour of the Continent. Twain plays with that ambiguity, especially when he is not on foot but riding in a carriage, taking a train, or sailing between shores. When he is tramping, he carries a pedometer, tries to sustain a steady gait, and enjoys the benefit of talking while walking. Despite what he declares to be "the true charm[s] of pedestrianism" (xxii,108), he frequently and mockingly rationalizes a decision to employ an alternate mode of transportation, calculating the savings in time and energy over simply tramping. Yet there is some arduous tramping throughout. He and his partner make extended enjoyable excursions through the Black Forest and elsewhere, thankfully sometimes even downhill, along with strenuous climbs up hills and mountains and miles of footing it on the level. Like Bunyan's *Pilgrim's Progress* or Bryson's *A Walk in the Woods* or a slew of manuals and guides on the joys of hiking, *A Tramp Abroad* sets out to be a tramp but time, pleasure, and variety, even necessity, dictate other modes of travel for Twain and his companion, Mr. Harris. At one point, the envy of passengers on a cog train prompts a change in how the summit is addressed. Twain argues, with humorous effect, that a carriage drawn by spirited horses will save time and patience. Another time he concludes that a boat is the only sensible means of navigating directly to a site on the other side of a lake.

Alternatives to tramping spare the pair of travelers (or tramps) encounters with beggars and riff-raff on the road. Etcetera. When the itinerary enfolds the prospect of "a considerable walk, from Lucerne to Interlaken, over the Brunig Pass," it is shunted, for "at the last moment the weather was so good that I changed my mind and hired a four-horse carriage. It was a huge vehicle, roomy, as easy in its motion as a palanquin, and exceedingly comfortable" (xxxi,159). The sightseeing that it afforded is lyrically recorded:

> We . . . went bowling over a hard, smooth road, through the summer loveliness of Switzerland, with near and distant lakes and mountains before and about us for the entertainment of the eye, and the music of multitudinous birds to charm the ear. Sometimes there was only the width of the road between the imposing precipices on the right and the clear cool water on the left with its shoals of uncatchable fishes skimming about through the bars of sun and shadow; and sometimes, in place of the precipices, the grassy land stretched away, in an apparently endless upward slant, and was dotted everywhere with snug little chalets, the peculiarly captivating cottage of Switzerland. (xxxi,159-60)

The text is embellished with a sketch by the author demonstrating the difference between new and old styles of cottage architecture; the traditional alpine version, of course, is made to appear more appealing.

The climb up Mount Riffleberg stands out as an expedition as fanciful as the voyages of Gulliver. The scale is preposterous, the procession numbering 154 men and fifty-one animals, principally mules but also a small herd of cows. In addition to the author and Mr. Harris, self-appointed leaders of the group, the entourage comprises seventeen guides, four surgeons, three chaplains, a botanist, a geologist, fifteen barkeepers, and even a Latinist. Among the subordinates are waiters, a half-dozen cooks, a barber, a butler, and various other assistants. The rations, epic in quantity, include sixteen cases of hams, two barrels of flour, twenty-two barrels of whiskey, 2,000 cigars, and 143 pairs of crutches (just in case). They tote much gear: twenty-five spring mattresses, twenty-nine tents, 154 umbrellas, twenty-two tall ladders, ninety-seven ice axes, two miles of rope, and five cases of dynamite. Indisputably, the cavalcade, comments the author, "was the most imposing expedition that had ever marched from Zermatt" (xxxvii,202). Strung out single file and roped together, it measured 3,122 feet in length—each member attired in evening dress, wearing blue goggles and toting a walking stick, an umbrella, a coil of rope, an ice-ax, and crutches. As a flourish, "the burdens of the pack mules and the horns of the cows were decked with Edelweiss and Alpine rose[s]" (xxxvii,203). Spectators were agog! Conducted as if it were a celebrated battalion at war, the ascent ensured difficulties of all sorts: the stealthy departure of the guides, a mutiny among the dispirited and fatigued men, the loss of a member of the party who fell to his death, and the error-prone thermometer and other instruments that made it impossible to certify that they had gotten to the summit elevation.

The descent, too, is comic. Hilariously, the first plan involves using umbrellas to parachute down, but no one volunteers to test the proposition. The leaders, Twain and Harris, consulting a guidebook, are convinced that they should be able to make their way down in considerably less time than it took to scale the mountain. The umbrella scheme scrapped, Plan B was to ride the glacier down. Imagine! When after a couple of hours of an apparent stall, it was calculated that the ice was moving at best at a rate of speed or slowness that would entail nearly five-hundred years for the return trip, the baggage at the outer edge arriving even "some generations later" (xxxix,222), Plan C kicks in. They surmise that, in lieu of being conveyed an inch a day on the ice, the party should be able to walk the distance in at most several days. Deliberations over, the decision is made.

The episode of scaling Riffleberg is a high point (both literally, with its elevation of 5,000 plus feet, and imaginatively, in its development as a comic fiasco). The descent is as outrageous as the ascent. The spoof here is on formulating hypotheses and using scientific equipment. Adding to the overall humor and satire, upon sterilizing his thermometer and barometer, Twain discovers that they serendipitously produce a deliciously edible soup and, simultaneously, that the climbers can make necessary corrections to the elevation readings. Twain states: "I boiled my thermometer, and sure enough, this spot, which purported to be 2,000 feet higher than the locality of the hotel, turned out to be 9,000 feet *lower*. Thus the fact was clearly demonstrated, that, *above a certain point, the higher a point seems to be, the lower it actually is*. Our ascent itself was a great achievement, but this contribution to science was an inconceivably greater matter" (xxxviii,216). We could just as well be in the company of Gulliver, the model empiricist portrayed by Swift. And to cap it off, Twain becomes so enamored of the soup, he "ordered the cook to have barometer soup every day" (xxxviii,210), a staple for the group.

Another farce recounted is an absurd, elaborately prepared French duel that astonishingly ends not as dreaded. Twain comically presents evidence of the senseless behavior of ants, celebrates a realm where manure constitutes the asset of greatest value, and lards the narrative with a host of incredible legends. The book is thick with outlandish stories. While the tall tales don't appear to exhibit aspects of travel, they provoke laughter, which is the motive for Twain's writing the book. Fake explanations are also a source of the risible. Take, for example, Twain's excuse for not precariously lying down to gauge the depth of a precipice: "I did not do this," he explains, "because I did not wish to soil my clothes" (xxxv,186). He celebrates the ease and economy of climbing a mountain by way of a telescope and not having to truck with guides and tons of equipment. Twain favors the telescope route for climbing Mont Blanc, the loftiest mountain in Europe. "Going by telescope" (xliv, 247), incidentally, gives a new, undoubtedly unique definition to armchair traveling, I might add.

The failure to reach the top of Rigi-Kulm (at 6,000 feet) to witness the gorgeous sunrise is also a comic triumph. The ridiculous mix-up over wrong times, the pair repeatedly getting up mid-morning instead of at the crack of dawn, and the finale of their making it to the summit but mistaking a sunset for sunrise by confusing p.m. for a.m. compound the comedy of errors. Totally preposterous, the story rides on the comic rails of miss-timing, pretended naivety, puffed-up seriousness, exaggerated mannerisms, and mock lamentations when things go wrong.

In the same vein, Twain enjoys making fun of German customs. He lays out an elaborate anecdote, denying all the while that it was fictitious, to explain the origin behind so many Germans wearing glasses. As to the politeness of greeting passersby, he admits: "We had taken a good deal of trouble to teach ourselves the kindly German custom of saluting all strangers with doffed hat, and we resolutely clung to it, that morning, although it kept us bareheaded most of the time and was not always responded to" (xxxiv, 180). Again, in advocating German ways, Twain appears to go along with the extreme claims made for the medicinal and social benefits of bathing in natural springs or spas but does so by raising the panegyric to comic heights.

All travelers naturally compare people, practices, things, and customs back home with those they run into in foreign lands. In *A Tramp Abroad*,

Twain also invokes differences in comic effects. The topic of food, for instance, becomes a laughing point when Twain contrasts European fare and American plenty. Tired of foreign foods and longing for American favorites, he lists nearly a hundred dishes he plans to indulge in as soon as he returns. Speaking of the relativity of tastes, he muses that while he might praise the food back home, "the Scotchman would shake his head and say, 'Where's my haggis?' and the Fijian would sigh and say, 'Where's your missionary?'" (xlix, 278-79). He concludes his comparison of menus with some comically bogus recipes.

In *A Tramp Abroad*, Twain is up to high jinks and pranks at every turn. Count on it, whether he is describing an imprint of a camel's foot as "a track in the dust like a pie with a slice out of it" (xlix, 278-79) or exclaiming on camel dung used for frescos on an otherwise unadorned hut or stored as fuel for cooking and heat. Other subjects arrayed for comic undermining have to do with pathetic disabled beggars in the streets of Constantinople, the classic lines of the columns supporting the Parthenon, a bold escapade in Spain, a nearly disastrous haircut and shave in Paris, and a snag over a lost passport in Russia. Twain, in *Innocents Abroad*, is the expert guide who sports a wink in the eye and can be counted on to have an apt, often funny comparison or witty retort ready on the tongue. He keeps the reader enthralled, generously filled in on details, and always looking forward to the next stop. In *A Tramp*, Twain relinquishes the guide's function of informing the would-be traveler of the particulars and takes on the role of the lead humorist. Here he is the King Midas of humor, as raconteur and purveyor of the outrageous. The levity of the tale carries over to a series of satirical appendices concerning such matters as—tongue-in-cheek—"The Awful German Language," the status of the European hotel *portier*, and the incomparable German newspapers.

While Twain is popularly and rightly most revered for his enticing tales of boyhood adventures, *Tom Sawyer* (1876) and *Huck Finn* (1884), he also made his mark as a travel writer. In *Life on the Mississippi* (1883), Twain, at the helm of a steamboat, studies the river banks, discovering that each side is different going down from what it is going back up. On the way to becoming an expert pilot, the novice celebrates life on and along the river. In *Roughing It* (1872), the spaciousness and wild character of the land, the excitement of prospectors and cowboys, and the folly of expecting laws and civilized conventions to obtain, all smothered in playful humor and rugged realism, is at the forefront. Twain's two accounts of travels in Europe—*The Innocents Abroad* (1870), a travelogue, and *A Tramp Abroad* (1880), a tale of travel more made-up than accurate—consist of the same ingredients. However, their respective recipes call for different proportions. In the former, adherence to the geography and history of the journey, spiced with humor, drives the account. In the latter, the madcap dominates, and, except for its broad trajectory, the journey recedes—places, persons, and encounters being distinguished by far-fetched elaborations bordering on the surreal and absurd.

FOLLOWING IN BUNYAN'S FOOTSTEPS

- *Pilgrim's Progress* -

The Pilgrim's Progress is a classic. The work has fascinated and inspired readers for centuries since it was penned by John Bunyan while in a jail cell back in the 17th century. Its itinerary and landscape form an archetype of the Christian life and palpably reinforce biblical precepts and parallels. If not in its entirety, at least lengthy passages from the book were often well-known to the point of being memorized. Early on, it became a bestseller. Nowadays, the volume is thought by non-readers to be old-fashioned, obsolete in both its language and its concept of devoting one's life to traveling to the celestial city. (Readers familiar with *Pilgrim's Progress* will recognize echoes of its theme and aspects of its plot and landscape in Jude's vision of Christminster as the city of his heavenly dreams, in Thomas Hardy's *Jude the Obscure*, as well as countless allusions to it in other works, notably in Mark Twain's *Innocents Abroad*.)

While *Pilgrim's Progress* is a must for those who aim to be culturally literate, it is a treat for those who crave adventure in travel literature. For it is action-packed with graphic on-the-road mishaps and scrapes. A piece of travel literature, the book to boot is a magnificent example of allegory. As an orientation, before making our way on the pilgrimage with Bunyan, it is best to recap our knowledge of Allegory. Quite simply, allegory attempts to give flesh-and-blood representation to truisms. Not only persons but objects, actions, and even features of the landscape are intended to carry meanings already appreciated outside the work by those reading or hearing the narrative, seeing the drama performed, or examining the painting or sculpture. Allegory depends on a system of cross-references. The allegorist uses imaginative figures to express truths about human nature and behavior.

Moral abstractions are embodied in fictional characters whose actions comprise the plot or storyline and, together with the dialogue, provide the dynamics of the ideological scheme or set of beliefs informing the work. The characters are personifications of abstract ideas, such as Love, Faith, or Despair. The dramatic focus is twofold: our attention is caught both by the story and by its considerable significance, the application it has for our lives. The interplay of these two centers of attention supplies fascination and meaning. In short, to navigate allegory is to follow two levels of interest or involvement simultaneously: the superficial plot connections between characters in action and the significance of all this activity on the level of ideas. In an allegory, we keep track of what is happening and register the associated moral principles being advanced.

Many commentators have praised Bunyan for his homely, animated colloquial style. Representative of the narrator's comfortable prose is a passage near the beginning when Christian, Bible in hand and pack on his back, has set forth on his quest for the heavenly city, encouraged by Evangelist and having just encountered and successfully dealt with Pliable and Obstinate. "Now as *Christian* was walking solitary by himself," writes Bunyan,

> he espied one afar off come crossing over the field to meet him; and their hap was to meet just as they were crossing over the way of each other. The gentleman's name that met him was Mr. *Worldly Wiseman:* he dwelt in the Town of *Carnal Policy*, a very great Town, and also hard by from whence *Christian* came. This man then meeting with *Christian*, and having some inkling of him,—for Christian's setting forth from the City of *Destruction* was much noised abroad, not only in the Town where he dwelt, but also it began to be the town-talk in some other places,—Master *Worldly Wiseman* therefore, having some guess of him, by beholding his laborious going, by observing his sighs and groans, and the like, began thus to enter into some talk with *Christian*. (21)

Intriguing dialogue and exposition ensue.

Throughout, the dialogue flows like good gossip. The speeches of Interpreter, Talkative, Ignorance, By-Ends, Faithful, and a host of minor characters are vividly depicted and frequently ear-perking. They also signal whether the speaker is on the right or wrong path. Though now archaic, certain phrases still suggest an idiomatic briskness. I'm thinking of "they made a pretty good shift to wag along" (306) or "'Look. . . . How far yonder youngster loitereth behind'" (148). Many phrases are still current: "if he could pick out the meaning" (113), "not to trouble his head" (44), "had like to a been" (118,193), "'Right, you hit it'" (311), "He had half a thought to go back" (68). And what sounds more natural than Mr. Contrite's remark: "In *those* days we were afraid to walk the Streets, but *now* we can shew our heads" (284). That we could be so fortunate, you say! Of course, some images and locutions are as foreign as the King James Bible: "Gird up his loins" (32, 41), "setting thy feet in that way that leadeth unto" (27), or "he verily thought" (68). It is about like reading Shakespeare.

To my mind, the Second Part seems more realistic than the First Part in its choice of every day, even domestic images. The shift is mainly due to Christian's wife and their four children having become the pilgrims. References to common animals, sewing, courtship, marriage and pregnancy, coaches and inns, and the like abound. References to such unlikely things as monsters and giants, whose heads, incidentally, really begin rolling in the Second Part. But from beginning to end, allegory and realism are deftly blended. Slowest going are those segments that are pure catechisms, such as the dialogue between Christian and Ignorance. The host of personages and the myriad places encountered by Christian and later by his family make for a most interesting and memorable journey. Near the close of the Second Part, like a coda, Valiant-for-Truth ticks off the difficulties of the pilgrimage. In fact, given that Christian and persons who join him share accounts of their adventures at various points along the way, the reader is conveniently presented with intermittent summaries of the sequence of episodes and the respective impact on the travelers.

The book's geography leaves an indelible impression on readers as they accompany the protagonist on his pilgrimage. Bunyan's descriptions of topography are endowed with double force, allowing one to observe the landscape as both a literal feature and an externalized projection of the given spiritual state of the pilgrim and other travelers on the road. The importance of embarking on and sticking to the right way with dispatch is dramatized at the outset, when Christian is seen defying family and friends, even plugging his ears to avoid their protestations, and looking straight ahead, single-mindedly pursuing his pilgrimage. Noting that "The Neighbors also came out to see him run" (15), Bunyan captures the simple urgency and newsworthy oddity of "a brain-sick fellow" convinced he must flee his hometown as a city of destruction and set out for the Wicket-Gate, the portal to the celestial city. By not going or turning back or off the road to salvation, this traveler and all others jeopardize their souls' chances of reaching heaven and will surely wind up in perdition. The route outlined in *Pilgrim's Progress* is a phantasmagoria marked with misleading milestones, fatiguing vagaries of terrain, and threatening occupants; the way is everywhere fraught with distractions, alluring detours, and puzzling crossroads. Those who travel there constantly have to be alert to find the right direction to follow. They must contend with the Slough of Despond and keep a sharp eye on the Wicket-Gate, emblematic of the target. They need to pass through the Valley of the Shadow of Death and make it beyond Vanity Fair to the Delectable Mountains and beyond to the river and orchard to receive succor and refreshment for their weary selves and souls. Christian and Hopeful trudge onward and, midway before the bleak episode at the Doubting Castle and within two miles of the goal, in sight of the golden city, and hearing the heavenly bells, trumpets, and chorus of hymns and praise, enter the Country of Beulah. Then they (and all who complete the pilgrimage) ford the river in which they must relinquish their mortal garments in preparation for the transfiguration promised the faithful. The pilgrimage is arduous, but the prize for persevering is worth it.

Pilgrim's challenge is to stay on the straight and narrow path and not get sidetracked. But like any wayfarer, he meets trouble on and off the road, and it is a struggle to keep going and make it to the destination. He must negotiate mountains and hills, valleys, and swamps and overcome monsters, troublemakers, and hardships that distract him and take a toll on his stalwart persistence to keep the faith and reach the end mapped out for him. His itinerary, the terrain he is traversing, and the persons and figures he bumps into along the way are both realistic and allegorical. But what we comprehend as symbolic is real for Christian. Because the story is told as if in a dream, however, it often appears to us as surreal or fantastic.

Structurally, Bunyan likens his story to a dream. From time to time, the narrator refers to dream fragments as the source of his tale. The story of Part I fittingly ends when the narrator awakens: "So I awoke, and behold it was a Dream" (167). On the title page, he writes: *"The Pilgrim's Progress from This World to That Which Is to Come,"* adds, *"Delivered Under the Similitude of a Dream,"* and goes on to note what the tale depicts, namely, *"Wherein Is Discovered the Manner of His Setting Out, His Dangerous Journey, and Safe Arrival at the Desired Country."* He follows the full title with an epigraph, in this case, a quotation from Scripture: "'I have used similitudes.' Hosea 12:10." The word *similitude* means "likeness," "parable," or, to pick up on something we defined earlier, "allegory." The notion of the dream helps allow for the distortions and oddities that crowd the narrative. It's an appeal to our credulity. The genre of a dream vision is coupled with allegory. Together they afford the author a way of presenting the dichotomy of the other world and this world. The work becomes a sustained parable, a more straightforward, down-to-earth way to convey something complex and spiritual. The physical state mirrors the spiritual state.

A state of being, a mood, for instance, despair, is pictured as a physical entity. The most famous of the landscape features depicted in *Pilgrim's Progress* is the Slough of Despond. The picture of the man sitting in an iron cage of despair is of rival clarity. Elsewhere a "hill is called *Difficulty*" (45), and in another place, a hill is known as Error. "The highway up which *Christian* was to go was fenced on either side with a Wall, and that Wall is called Salvation" (41). Near it "stood a Cross, and a little below in the bottom, a Sepulcher" (41-42), into which the pilgrim's burden "loosed from off his shoulders . . . tumble[d]" (42) and disappeared. Like all pilgrims, all persons, that is, Christian has to make it through the Valley of the Shadow of Death. As long as Pilgrim ponders heaven and keeps aware of his ultimate destination, Mount Zion, he can continue making progress on his arduous journey. He has to stay focused despite innumerable distractions or—in the logo of the pilgrimage—temptations and setbacks. Things go well for Christian as long as he stays on course and remembers that he is taking "the King's High-Way, the way of Holiness" (63). When he forgets his trip's path and designated goal, a metaphor for life, he gets side-tracked and has to work harder to get back on track returning to the straight and narrow. Plenty of characters along the way, some masquerading as friends and proffering help, seek to keep him off course and lure him into danger. It's hard to be steadfast when there are so many appeals to his worldly senses and challenges to taking the rougher road.

Christian is beset by personages whose tag names say it all—Talkative, Mistrust, Atheist, Little-Faith, Ignorance, the Seven Deadly Sins, Superstition, Misters Hold-the-World, Money-love, Save-all, Gripe-man, and Love-gain. As is frequently the case in a make-believe adventure, he is attacked by dragons and beasts. He falters due to the difficult terrain as well. At times, understandably, Christian wanders from the path and succumbs to temptations, but being a good and faithful pilgrim, a dedicated traveler, he persists and reaches his destination. He follows his intended itinerary as best he can. He must not give in to those who deride him and call his pilgrimage a "desperate journey" (72). Christian has to keep going and remain resolute, even when it would be fun to while away his time at Vanity Fair and other places of perpetual earthly pleasure. By lingering, he would deprive himself of ultimate residence in the Celestial City. What a choice!

The Giant Despair, who lives in the Doubting Castle, from which Christian manages to escape once he remembers that he carries a key called Promise, which unlocks the doors, poses a significant threat. The nearly fatal fight with the dreaded dragon Apollyon in the Valley of Humiliation whets our suspense and gives cause to be concerned over the welfare of the protagonist. His miraculous recovery, however, does not embolden him for future victories. Thankfully, present and offsetting the dangers are safeguards and signs that keep Christian progressing: the roll he temporarily misplaces and returns to find, importantly, his certificate for entry into Mount Zion, the armor bestowed upon him at the Beautiful Palace by its generous residents, the cross upon which he contemplates the passion of the crucified Lord, and the true friends and the angelic company that serves to guide and cheer him on. Help in various forms plays a role in the Pilgrim's salvation.

Fortunately, he meets up with more than fair-weather friends to keep him going in the right direction, such as Evangelist, Good-Will, Prudence, Piety, Charity, "a grave and beautiful damsel, named Discretion" (51), and a neighbor with the name of Faithful. On the way, shortly after meeting "three sturdy rogues" (115) named Faint-heart, Mistrust, and Guilt, Christian and Hopeful notice how easily the rogues overtake Little-Faith, another traveler out there.

When asked by Christian whether he knew a guy named Temporary, Hopeful, his traveling companion for a stretch of the way, retorts, "'Know him! yes, he dwelt in *Graceless*, a town about two miles off of *Honesty*, and he dwelt next door to one *Turn-back*." That starts a discussion about why so many believers become backsliders. At the end of that conversation, the pilgrims find themselves at the outskirts of the heavenly Jerusalem. There, in the presence of a pair of angels on the other side of the river, they are led to the gate and final destination of their journey. Midst joyful music of bells, the pilgrims are welcomed in and transfigured, adorned in "raiment . . . that shone like gold" (166) and given harps, crowns, and palms for everlasting worship of God. Christian's journey and his arrival in heaven are the road map and destination for his wife and family, whose pilgrimage is the focus of the Second Part.

In reading the book, we, in effect, accompany him and his family, our surrogates and prototypes, on that self-same pilgrimage.

JUPITER CIRCLES THE EARTH

The narrative of Ted Simon's *Jupiter's Travels*, published in 1979, begins with a flash-forward. The motorcyclist is out of gas just outside Gaya, "the dirtiest town in India," waiting for help, having logged three years of his journey and finding that during the past several days, due to a miscalculation regarding the direction of the Ganges River, he had ridden one hundred and fifty miles farther from his destination, Calcutta. "Officially," as announced in the London *Sunday Times*, his 65,000-mile, four-year-long journey around the world "began at 6 p.m. on Saturday the sixth of October 1973" (17). All along the way, the narrator keeps the reader updated on his progress, citing the names of cities visited and in round figures reporting the mileage traveled—sometimes forecasting the length of anticipated time in hours or days to get there. Like a banquet meal savored in between courses, these summing-up sentences at strategic points in the text break up the journey into discrete segments. He supplements such check-off points with maps outlining stretches of the route section-by-section, country-and-continent-or-subcontinent-by-subcontinent.

At the outset, the appellation "Jupiter," a namesake commemorating a planet and a god, is conferred on Ted Simon, the narrator, in a session with a holy man at a Rajput wedding. Simon accepts the name, calling it "a lovely name . . . like cream and honey in the mouth" (418), and the concomitant challenges that it poses for its incarnation in him for the duration of his sweep around the globe. The circumstances surrounding the prophecy the holy man gave are detailed later when the epic chronicle catches up again in India. Fortunately, the bad luck predicted by the fortune teller, evinced by a couple of serious accidents, only occurs after the journey is completed and he is home again. Regardless of any public adulation over his feat, the narrator persistently eschews any posture of a hero. Yet, owing to the privileged knowledge and exalted view he gains on his worldwide travels, he believes he reaches a status tantamount to that of a god. The tale he tells is a coming of age of a grand sort, growth in consciousness and beneficence. Simon folds his arms around the whole of creation, humanity, the animals, the entire sphere of life and nature. He lamented the plight civilized humankind has brought on, a plight apparent in and exacerbated by the disharmony in the ascendant. He rues the misery and poverty he witnesses and sees it as a plight intensified by overpopulation and man's avaricious exploitation of nature. In this respect, *Jupiter's Travels* shares some affinities with the genre of sacred texts. Not apocryphal in its origins or its account, the book discloses an authentic journey around the world by a representative individual who is, as he avows mythically, "in search of immortality" and "truth" (404). The journey constitutes a "close interweaving of action and reflection." As he proclaims, riding his motorcycle across India, among strangers whose lives and situations were so conspicuously foreign to his, "I could imagine myself as a mythical being, a god in disguise that might pass their way only once in a lifetime" (401). While simultaneously enduring the throes and enjoying the pleasures and sporadic insights of the arduous journey he is making, he modestly admits he feels ineloquent and baffled rather than sagacious.

In getting ready for the trip, Simon only packs what he thinks will be essential. The different "departments" he stocks—"Food, Clothing, Bed, Tools, First Aid, Documents, Cameras and Fuel" (18)—are labeled as to their source, the rooms and locations in the house and garage where they permanently belong. Stuff transferred to the motorcycle is remembered as Kitchen, Bedroom and Wardrobe, Workshop, and Office. Things that couldn't be categorized fit under Miscellaneous. Items of clothing and articles stashed in his "medical arsenal" are all inventoried, and their inclusion is justified or rationalized. All had to fit on the bike. Daunting is the task of narrowing down the list of what to take. Planning is largely a matter of thinking of the diverse places he would visit and what would be needed there. By forecasting specific locations and peculiarities of weather and natural phenomena he would likely be encountering, he adroitly compiled a list of necessities.

The traveler's departure to the unknown is a succession of good-byes to the known—family and friends, London, and all the sights on the way to Dover. Beginning in Europe, the initial leg of the journey takes him expeditiously from London through France and Italy, mostly passing through familiar haunts, to the ferry boat for Tunis. The sections entitled "Africa" and "Falling and Rising," taking up 150 pages, over a third of the book, commence in Tunisia and move on through Libya and Egypt, where he dreads border police will turn him away. His ride continues along the southern Mediterranean seacoast and southward through Ethiopia, Kenya, Tanzania, Zambia, Rhodesia, and thence to South Africa. The section entitled "America" picks up from Brazil, following a voyage in a cargo ship from Mozambique, and traces a meandering 10,000-mile route first south and next north through South America, up to Central America and Mexico, and on to California, a point 6,000 miles after landing in an airport in Panama. Closing the chapter in his life spent at a commune in northern California, a stay spanning late summer and fall, he bids farewell to Carol, with whom he had lived and fallen in love. From San Francisco, he sails with his bike in tow to Australia. In the land down under, his explorations carry him from the northeast shore amidst rains and flooding rivers and washed-out roads down along the eastern and drier southern shores. From Perth in the southwest, he sails to Asia, spending time in Singapore and Malaysia before heading aboard a ferry boat for India.

By design, his ride is monumental. He covers a lot of ground from Bombay to Delhi, Kanpur, Calcutta, and the connecting cities, fishing towns, and countryside. His circuitous route includes Nepal, Bangladesh, and Pakistan. He keeps track of passing days on the calendar and accumulated mileage since leaving L.A. From New Delhi, he "shot up the trunk road to Amritsar like an arrow from a bow" (433). In places, he is forced to go slow to avoid competing with heavy traffic and to stay safe. Turkey and continental Europe he regards as spaces to get beyond, the last hurdles to leap to reach London and home. He has succumbed to fatigue and homesickness. He admits, "The urge to move westward was irresistible" (433).

The trip takes a toll on both bike and rider. Several times en route, the Triumph breaks down, gets a tire punctured, runs out of gas, blows a fuse, and calls for minor or major repairs, including piston replacements, overhauls, changing the spark plugs, and fixing or renewing forks, sprockets, and other critical parts. The roads don't help. Many miles of corduroy surface, steep grades to negotiate, fluctuations in temperature from intense heat to frigid cold, terrain morphing from sand to mud to rock, and other sometimes freaky obstacles compound the challenge of traversing undeniably lengthy expanses. In places, ruts are so deep the bike tips over. Often it is very slow going. At times, oncoming traffic, especially trucks, crowds the right-of-way and retards the progress, extending the difficulty of reaching desired locations in the expected time frame. To boot, the motorcycle is laden with provisions, gear, and spare parts. To upright it and repack it takes time and effort. Not to mention getting soaked from the frequent deluge of rains. Besides saturating his clothes, boots, and bedroll, the torrent wreaks havoc on matches, paper money, and pages of his journal. In addition to the ravages of the weather, there's always the threat of the motorcycle being stolen.

As with Pirsig, in *Zen and the Art of Motorcycle Maintenance*, Simon measures potential by the level of his gas tank. A full tank allows for three hours of traveling and indulging in thoughts both pleasant and unpleasant. Admittedly, he yields to bouts of fantasizing, letting his mind race ahead to imagine ominous hazards and prospects that could threaten to ruin or end the journey. Habitually the rider's frame of mind vacillates between hope and fear. The reader frequently receives an initially off-putting report of a place. As the traveler's knowledge of the place and its inhabitants and history increases, it is exchanged for a sympathetic or enticing view. The narrator has dreams and nightmares, literally and temperamentally, and is quick to share them. In tight spots where the outcome is unpredictable, he deliberately suppresses hope and expects the worst. When he's able to get past a border, manages to find a resting place, or makes it to a source for fuel or repairs or food and drink, he cheers up again.

The trip comes to an annoying standstill at the port city of Fortaleza, Brazil, where Simon is detained while his passport and certification papers are sent off to officials for verification. For several weeks matters stall. His motorcycle is impounded. He is incarcerated and not allowed to leave but is fed, given a cot to sleep on, and permitted to perambulate or, if he prefers, be chauffeured about the precincts. The narrative grinds to a halt, and the temperament of the narrator swings between collapse and hope. Both reader and narrator lose patience. The hiatus grates, despite being delineated in a well-written script and replete with graphic detail, albeit now and then bordering on the quotidian and repetitive. Consequently, the release is welcomed by the narrator and reader alike, the reader having served as a vicarious detainee in the process.

By contrast, his sojourn in a hippie colony in northern California—an experience only a little toned down from an equivalent in Kerouac—becomes a means of bringing out and reinforcing the narrator's aptitude and desire for surrendering to other modes of life than that of his pre- and post-trip life. What is so striking about the journey being told and accounts for the engagement the reader feels is the capacity of the narrator to become involved in the life and space at every junction and still retain a critical, almost solipsistic separateness or distance from it. Involved and detached—the dichotomy expressed in the ambiguity inherent in the narrator's complex response to his experiences on the journey contributes significantly to the truth and interest of the account.

Mental and physical stamina, ever vulnerable, are sorely tested on the solitary marathon trip. Simon notes, "On my journey I had scrupulously resisted travelling as though to a destination" (305). He discovered early on that by utilizing an ever-present focus on the moment, one can maximize the pleasure of time spent traveling. He fights against the thought of being done and strives, often in vain, to keep focused on the immediate moment and, at most, the next turn of the road or temporary stopping place to rest, eat, look around, and perhaps mingle with locals. Rather than fixate on completing the planned journey, seeing it as an ordeal or a goal to be reached, he comes to appreciate, a little belatedly, "that the interruptions *were* the journey" (132).

All does not go well on the journey. Simon is bitten in the foot by a crab, sustains an injury to his left eye from a back-lashed hook while fishing, has numerous mishaps on the road, and succumbs to colds, even hyperthermia, as well as an intense fever, headaches, and body aches and stiffness from incessant riding. As a relief from camping out, he occasionally strikes for a cheap hotel or, if lucky, benefits from the offer of overnight accommodations from someone he meets along the way—only on one such occasion suffering bites from bedbugs. Also, on the debit side, he loses his passport and wallet and wears out or loses some of his clothes, including his treasured flight jacket. But (as reflected in passages in italics that serve as soliloquies), he rallies himself to not capitulate to depression, even when an exceedingly rough patch is upon or ahead of him. He just lowers expectations and awaits the outcome, knowing he'll somehow make it through eventually. It is a battle to maintain equanimity. The road is not easy. Simon contends with all manner of natural forces, is beset by rain storms and extremes of temperature, and is now and again left to brave it alone in the presence of wild animals and violent men. Authority-wielding, gun-carrying border guards add complications, delay, and hostility to the challenges he confronts during bad weather while coping with inhospitable climate and barely navigable roads.

On the plus side, the scenery at points is gorgeous or impressive for its foreignness: endless deserts, savannahs, forests, foothills and mountains, lakes, rivers, coasts, and oceans. He takes it all in firsthand! He likens some of his experiences to "B" movies, others to "A" movies, but he revels in the knowledge that all is real, even if seemingly surreal. People he sees and meets in the different lands, strangers viewed from a distance and in throngs, people working in hotels and shops or there as guests, and many whom he becomes acquainted with or befriended—the album is full of pictures and experiences of life across the planet. Birds and animals, sun and stars, and clouds supply interest, color, variety, and subject matter for the panorama that is Jupiter's journey. A census of the animals he sees, those in their natural habitats and those harnessed or herded by men, comes close to resembling the passenger list from the animal kingdom aboard Noah's ark: camels, elephants, tigers, kangaroos, baboons, monkeys, hippos, deer, zebras, giraffes, sheep, llamas, cows, buffaloes, pigs, horses, mules, dogs, and cats; storks, pelicans, ostriches, albatrosses, eagles, and birds of all breeds and songs and flights and colors; fish and other sea creatures large and small. He is uplifted by the sight of wildlife but can't ignore that humans have systematically diminished and blighted much of the natural world.

His first view of wild elephants encapsulates the thrill of visiting Africa; it is a passage rivaling the writing of noted naturalists. He observes: "There were ten of them, about three hundred yards away, gathered close together under a tree. . . . They were nuzzled up to each other, wonderfully satisfying shapes, smooth and solid, superimposed in a cluster of curves; all the more alive for being so utterly still" (141-142). In the passage in which Simon discusses the encounter with the elephants and delineates their basic characteristics and appeal, he goes on to detail the name of the tree, a *baobab*, more popularly called the bottle tree, and its attributes, including the use of its leaves to make soup and its fruit to produce a drink. Also, he points out that while elephants are naturally grey, those he observes appear to be brown, which he explains is obviously due to the practice of dusting themselves. Simon is uplifted by witnessing the novelty of elephants at ease, acknowledging that he is seeing what many others have seen down through the ages. He is thus accorded a kinship with his predecessors. In fine, he regards the scene as emblematic of Africa and as a challenge to humankind to honor and preserve biodiversity. Resembling an apostrophe, the prose piece celebrating the elephants rises to its climax with a single exclamatory, all-encompassing word: *Africa*!

While he covers continental stretches of land on the bike, at speeds ranging from only a few mph to 70 or occasionally higher, conditions permitting, Simon uses waterways and airways to portage and stitch together the main pieces of the tapestry that is his journey. His trip encircling the globe necessitates transporting the motorcycle across oceans and seas to resume the road trip and advance on the determined route connecting islands and land masses of forty different countries.

People whom he meets are vividly described and become actors in the drama. He is not always on the go; there are interludes when he makes an extended visit or stay, mostly with strangers who are instantly willing and generous hosts and who become friends. Here and there, he looks up "friends of friends" to land on for a meal, a bed, a bit of companionship, and conversation. In northern California, he joins a group on a ranch with woods and gardens, a smattering of simple hand-wrought houses, and freedom from restrictive social conventions—where he, like the mariners in *The Odyssey*, is lulled into remaining in Lotos land, settles down, falls in love, and nearly relinquishes thought of finishing the ordeal and adventure of his worldwide journey.

About a year and a half into the journey, while negotiating with guards on the Bolivian border, Simon meets up with Bruno and Antoine, a pair of likable Frenchmen who also speak Spanish and happen to be going his way. The ensuing sequence runs to forty pages and lasts about three months. The men immediately form a friendship and a caravan. Bruno's "battered Renault van" (266) follows behind Simon's Triumph. They complete the journey through Peru, Ecuador, and Columbia, sharing the road, meals, overnight campsites, and conversation till the van peters out on one of the steep inclines in the Andes. Bruno and Ted then part ways, Antoine having left the trio at Lima. Bruno auctions off the van and its contents and says farewell to his erstwhile traveling companion. Both again solo but now enriched with recent memories, they resume their respective journeys. The trio of travelers had enjoyed an idyllic time together along the Pacific coast, where they fished and marveled at the banana plantations. High up in the mountains, the lives of Inca descendants, their llamas, and the eagles overhead gave new focus to the journey. This treat was not wasted on the reader either.

Sometimes a person he sees, a disabled or blind beggar or a man in a turban astride a camel, may be remembered solely as a silhouette. Other times a drama unfolds, as with several notorious "truckies" in Australia whom he finds engaging and helpfully road-smart. In the case of the barman on the ferry to Tunis, a detailed and amusing portraiture is drawn. His movements and attitude are comically rendered in an alliterative flight: "As he steered his bumptious body back to the bar, he kicked aside the out-stretched feet of sleeping Tunisians rather than walk around them" (38)—no question about who is in charge.

In Kenya, the narrator meets a kindred spirit, a fellow motorcyclist, a young man from New Zealand, who likewise is covering the continents over a period approaching four years. Simon is spellbound by the account of his counterpart's adventures, accidents, and nearly fatal encounters, but even though early in Simon's journey, he is not deterred from duplicating the derring-do of this forerunner. Elsewhere, with a stroke of the pen reminiscent of Dickens, Simon picks up on an epithet, describing a guard at the Egyptian border as "roly-poly," and after that repeatedly refers to him as "Roly-Poly," converting the adjective to a proper noun. Shades of *Pickwick Papers*! His trip, for the most part, strips away stereotypes. However, "in the land of *No hay*," he finds himself put off by "the daily grind of contact with the Latin American personality" (303). There are hundreds of brief characterizations, each calling on the painter to dip his brush anew.

The portraitures of countries and cities too are fresh and vivid. Athar, in Sudan, is "among the hottest places in the world" (80). A close-up of Los Angeles puts into perspective the real and the make-believe, especially after exposure to and involvement in diverse, genuine cultures across the globe. Particularly in India but elsewhere as well, he is overwhelmed by "examples of misery and death" (398), poverty, and sickness. An event puncturing the pleasure of mingling in a bazaar occurs when he sees three poor, barefoot little girls run over by a heavily loaded horse-drawn carriage, two being hurt and one killed in the accident. About Tanzania, he confesses with a tinge of regret that he learned next to nothing. In the desert of Libya, he encounters a scene of incongruous elements, old and new. From a primitive pole-tent made of hides, atop sporting a TV antenna and alongside a pair of gas containers, exited a man attired in cotton and wearing sandals. Next, he slid into a fancy Mercedes and roared off on the road next to which two camels and an airplane were secured. What a collage! Like all travelers, Simon has favorite cities and accrues a stock of both fond and repulsive memories. Some foods stand out for their novelty and foreignness and are a treat for the palate; others make him sick. The diets, how people are attired, the various customs—all bespeak a journey abroad.

The book is a kaleidoscope and keeps changing with the motion of the journey. There are romps of lovemaking, though the narrator avoids the advances of whores. Beggars are nearly ubiquitous. When riding a solitary road and even among, maybe as a consequence of, crowds, Simon experiences times of lonely tedium. Not only the sights but the sounds and smells noted throughout attest to the authenticity of the travels. An amusing anecdote calling on auditory imagery targets a roommate in an African hotel called the Oilfield Hotel, where Simon spends a week. Except for one night, he is the sole occupant. The exception is the night the room is shared with a cook who exhibited "the loudest snore I have ever heard. In the night I throw everything at him, but the express trains continue to roar in and out of his nostrils" (55). Another off-putting sound accompanies the habit of spitting. Comments Simon, "The hawking and spitting, which is a constant background murmur to

Arab life, here rises to become the dominant sound, louder than speech, louder than the ferry's engine" (76). Nor is it pleasant to realize too late that one has shaken the left hand of an Arab, that being the appendage customarily used to wipe after a bowel movement. At times the narrator commiserates with Gulliver and also Alice in Wonderland. On the trip, reading *Walden*, he admires the closeness to nature celebrated by Thoreau and sees connections with some types of life and habitat he witnesses on his far-flung journey.

In ready response to Simon's introspective nature and straightforward and engaging style, and because the book covers such a length of time and space—four years and sixty-five thousand miles—and incorporates vast differences in cultural and geographical conditions, the reader becomes closely attached to the narrator. Caught up in the journey, it is as if the reader is riding in tandem with the narrator. Obviously, there is no possibility of riding on the protagonist's bike; it is already overloaded with gear and laboring under stress. As Jupiter rumbles along, taking in the scenes reeling by as in a movie, he shares the experience of an unusual sensation of movement: "I am a world spinning through visible time" (53). Elsewhere, reminiscent of Conrad, he likens his journey to "floating on a raft . . . back to the beginning of time" (109). Dwarfed by ever-changing, incomprehensible surroundings, he pictures himself as "this human speck making his snail's track across the floor of a vast arena" (177). *Jupiter's Travels* is bounded by mythic dimensions.

Unlike Naipaul or Theroux, Simon doesn't delve into political contexts or pursue and comment on religious issues. By contrast with the writing, say, of Bryson or Twain, in Simon's tale of travel, the use of humor is more sparing—present, but less conspicuous and more subtle. The style is lively, and the language is brimming with figurative flourishes, including scores of apt, uniquely expansive similes and metaphors. Embedded in the text like diamonds of varying cut and size, they add color and clarity, lighting up and refracting the meaning and artistry inherent in the narrative and compounding the interest readers seek and find in this account of an adventurist motorcyclist meandering around the entire globe. Not gaudy, the literary gems enrich the setting and advance aspects of the work, great and small, contributing insight, detail, and nuance, without which the work would surely be the plainer.

The dialogue is chatty, and word choice, from semiformal to colloquial and slang, like arrows pulled from a well-stocked quiver by a marksman sure of his target, is everywhere convincing. The book is both encyclopedic in scope and exciting in content. For sheer adventure, bounty of information, detailed tailoring of characterization, build-up of suspense, moments of self-introspection, and power of description and order of presentation, *Jupiter's Travels* is superb and holds the reader's attention from start to finish.

HOMER'S *THE ODYSSEY*

The Odyssey is an ancient Greek epic chronicling a hero's adventures on his homeward voyage to Ithaca after the Trojan War. It is an interweaving of three story-lines: the wanderings of Odysseus (Books 1 and 5-13), the search by Telemachus, Odysseus' son, for his father (Books 2-4), and Penelope's bouts with a host of eager suitors, their defeat and demise by her disguised, belatedly returned husband, and the couple's reunion (Books 14-24).

Epics, by nature, are episodic—adventure reigns. Odysseus encounters the Lotus-Eaters, fights with Cyclops, a one-eyed giant, and is several times actually or nearly shipwrecked. He sees his men transformed into pigs by an enchantress named Circe and visits dead persons, including his mother. He barely escapes the lures of sirens and later an attack by sea monsters. For seven years, he sojourns on an island with Calypso but ultimately makes it home to out-shoot and—with his mighty bow—kill the interlopers who came courting his wife during his long absence. The pace of epics is leisurely, and digressions within their loose narrative framework abound. We lose our way if we get impatient at the conventions and wish only to get on with the story in a straightforward manner. If it is simply fast food we crave, we will not enjoy a leisurely dinner or get absorbed in engaging conversation.

Other marks or conventions of an epic include catalogs, invocations to the muses, epithets, lengthy similes, monologues, formal speeches, debates, and councils. Besides verbal features, epics abound in activities and interventions of supernatural beings, the performance of religious rites (such as libations, sacrifices, and prayers), and the observance of omens and prophecies. Characteristic too are displays of hospitality, exchanges of gifts, feats, contests of strength, warfare, and, of course, a pervasive focus on the exploits and accomplishments of the hero. An epic is a poem celebrating a people's culture and the embodiment in the hero of its virtues and ideals.

In *The Odyssey*, several forces contend for control of a person's destiny. What happens may be the outcome of what the gods decree, what an individual does, how the person's character or will direct the consequences, or some other force or agency acting on behalf of or despite the person's interest. A person's fortune or plight may be the result of a combination of factors, including luck. Or the explanation of the cause may be dependent on the perspective taken. Consider what Zeus says early on, at the gathering of the gods at his palace in Olympia: "'Ah how shameless—the way these mortals blame the gods. / From us alone, they say, come all their miseries, yes, / but they themselves, with their own reckless ways, / compound their pains beyond their proper share'" (1,37-40).

The gods play an influential role in the lives and destinies of the Greeks. In Homer's depiction of them, humans and gods differ in the level of control and longevity but resemble each other in their propensity to take sides and indulge emotions. The relationship between Odysseus and the gods, goddesses, and other creatures of supernatural power is an intriguing aspect of the tale. He is both helped and hindered by them. Humans are not entirely autonomous, not even the ever-resourceful hero of the story. Odysseus' character is revealed, developed, and strengthened through his dealings with the various personages he encounters en route to Ithaca. The obstacles to his return become a means of proving the heroic stuff of Odysseus. They also represent the gods' retaliation for the Greeks' dishonoring Athena's temple and their treatment of Cassandra, King Priam's daughter. As the tale unfolds and we get swept up in the conflict, we acknowledge and distinguish between the anger of Athena and that of Poseidon and side with and rally the hero on his zigzagging way to triumph. Poseidon has it in for Odysseus because the warrior blinded the giant cyclops Polyphemus, offspring of Poseidon by a nymph. Athena, however, has a change of heart and even goes to bat for him at an assembly in Olympus at which the rest of the gods and goddesses are present. Both immortal creatures intervene in Odysseus' monumental quest to reach his homeland—one, ruler over the sea, impeding and vigorously attempting to thwart his return, the other empathetically and with creative powers succeeding in relieving the homebound hero of some of the impediments to his return and trying to hasten his voyage back to Ithaca. Athena is likewise instrumental in working out aspects of Odysseus' victory over the unruly suitors and, earlier, in aiding Telemachus in the search for his father's whereabouts.

Often Homer's descriptions are realistic and believable, other times far-fetched. But throughout, they are never lacking in vividness. A prime example is the account of the "Slaughter in the Hall" (Book 22), the culmination of the epic tale. It is impossible not to get swept up in all the intrigue and adventure, notwithstanding potential issues that arise as we read and ponder portions of the story—as, for instance, reconciling Odysseus' love for his wife and his relationships with the women he meets on his trip (Circe, Calypso, and Nausicaa). Though central to the theme and impact of *The Odyssey*, the sheer length of time it takes for the hero to make it back from the war calls on the willing suspension of disbelief. As do the methods the long-suffering wife employs to keep the obnoxious suitors at bay, the challenge she gives the lot of them who seek her hand in marriage, and the strength of hope she holds for her husband's eventual return. Even the divinely inspired subterfuge of the hero prior to revealing his identity upon returning to his home is a mix of contrivance and denouement. Yet, in the end, all such matters pale or fall into place as the narrative completes its course.

One turn of the story that bears on the hope of completing the homeward journey is the premature opening of a windbag by Odysseus' suspicious and covetous crew while he sleeps. They are in sight of their homeland when the disaster occurs. The gift from Aeolus, intended as a force in reserve should unfavorable sailing conditions prevail, becomes, in the distrustful hands of the mortals, a cursed device. Let loose, the winds reverse the mileage laboriously gained and not only double the travel time and extend the waves to be negotiated to reach the home shores again but also result in further obstacles. What a lamentable setback! The timing could not have been worse. The incident dramatizes the folly of mortals and the fate or bad luck that accompanies their bad choices and concomitantly bedevils another's good intentions. The incident triggers a series of protracted slowdowns and detours that beset the hero and add to the epic nature of the voyage that came to be called an odyssey.

The ill-timed release of the winds adds complications to Odysseus' journey home. The epic, having reached the length of nine adventure-packed books, at the start of the tenth, finds the hero, tantalizingly close to being home, flung back to Aeolia, where he had received the gift intended as a boon to his sail homeward. To get to where he had been again, at the shore of Ithaca, Odysseus is subjected to many obstacles and challenges that tie up Books 10 through 12. Boomeranged, he and his crew are chased out of Aeolia as personae non grata. Shortly thereafter, he loses most of his men to giant cannibals and is left with but one ship from his fleet. On another island, they idle away for over a year in the company of the goddess Circe in drug-induced forgetfulness, half of his enthralled men first being transformed into pigs. Advantaged by Hermes' gift of an herb to make him immune to her potion, Odysseus talks the pretty enchantress and captor into un-pigging his men.

Before they leave, however, she gives orders that they are to visit the land of the dead. In the dreaded journey within a journey, he encounters Teiresias and other legendary personages and familiar faces, including his own mother and the mother of Oedipus. He is updated on events back on the home front. When Circe comes to greet Odysseus and compliment him on his achievement, she tells him he is unique in that he alone among men is destined to die twice. She bids him and his men adieu and promises them protection but warns Odysseus of the navigational dangers he'll encounter in the form of the bewitching Sirens and, following that, the dreaded Scylla and Charybdis, between whose two rocks he must gingerly steer his ship to avoid the reach of the terrible monsters. They pass through, but with a toll of six lost comrades to the jaws of Scylla. Subsequently, landing on the Island of the Sun, warned by the blind prophet not to feast on the cattle there, Odysseus' men, their store of provisions depleted, defy their leader and, in a mutinous moment while he sleeps, capture, roast, and eat some of the forbidden cattle. After a week's feasting, the crew takes to the sea again. Storm and shipwreck, repercussions from the act of disobedience to the gods, ensue, and Odysseus, the sole survivor, struggles to shore on the island of Ogygia, home of the goddess Calypso and Lord Alcinous. Stung by the woeful tale of his guest, Alcinous offers a manned ship to escort him to Ithaca.

The second half of the epic, encompassing Books 13 through 24, recounts Odysseus' arrival in Ithaca. There he passes the test of strength, dramatized by his successful stringing and shooting of the legendary bow. The debacle of the suitors being slaughtered justly follows the exposure of their ill intentions and their exploitation of Odysseus' domain. The epic ends in a domestic victory, a culminating test of knowledge confirmed and documented by the hero's memory of the couple's unique bedstead, proof that Odysseus is rightfully home and is the legitimate husband of Penelope.

On journeys, however well planned, travelers encounter delays and surprises. Indeed, contingencies are often devised to anticipate and accommodate the unknown and spontaneous, frequently even welcomed additions or changes to the itinerary, the seemingly inevitable interruptions, delays, or missed goals caused by exigencies of travel. An epic, by definition, is a saga episodic and far-flung in scope. *The Odyssey* is the archetypal journey testing the stamina and resourcefulness of the traveler, proving whether he or she is up to the mark, ready and able to return and resume activities and life at home, the wiser and more appreciative for having taken and survived the trip.

It can be fun and refreshing to leave the ordinary and the commonplace and encounter novelty and strangeness, to depart from the familiar and the routine in favor of the foreign and the exceptional. That, after all, is the motivation for pursuing tales of travel. We read to journey somewhere, to satisfy our longing to be elsewhere. In reading *The Odyssey*, we learn a lot about the ancient Greeks' social structures, various lifestyles, and values. Granted, it is a world away from our present situation. Nevertheless, it offers much that continues to be universal about human nature. The knowledge we gain and the adventure we share account in large part for the immense and long-lasting popularity of the book. Our world is more extensive for our having traveled back in time to the distant ports and mythic moments visited in this epic story by Homer.

A TRIP INTO THE CONGO

- Penetrating the *Heart of Darkness* -

Conrad's *Heart of Darkness* is a story that works at several levels at the same time. In the first place, it is a tale of adventure and exploration. A young man takes off from home and goes abroad. He travels from England to Europe and the distant continent of Africa. It is a book about leaving home. When you leave home and encounter new places and different people, you naturally compare the past and the present, the familiar world back home with the new scene. Along with Marlow, the narrator of the story, we discover and expand our horizons and knowledge of the world and ourselves. Literally, without traveling a mile from where we now sit with a book in hand, we venture forth to gain an international perspective while enjoying a tale of intrigue and travel.

As Marlow's story unfolds, it is as if we are passengers on the *Nellie*, a sailboat at rest on the River Thames on the London waterfront in the early evening, awaiting the turning of the tide. We share a seat and listen as he recounts his tangled adventure and tries to fathom its depth and meaning. As we become engrossed in the mystery, excitement, and outcome of the tale, however low-key and disjointed in its telling, and struggle to keep up with the serpentine itinerary, we identify with Marlow and relive a part of his life. We are transported from our limited world to the wider world that Marlow explores. The story imparts knowledge. We learn geography and history, but we mostly learn about human experience and potential. *Heart of Darkness* is like the fruit of the forbidden tree in the Garden of Eden. It is a means for discovering the nature of good and evil and attempting to assess their limits. Conrad's intent, through the character Marlow, his mouthpiece, through the vehicle of a novel, is to shed light on the truth. In Marlow, Conrad projects his own experience of a trip to the Congo and ultimately gives us a modern Everyman. As we accompany the mariner-narrator on his journey, we define our fate and that of all human beings.

The story is a growth experience. On a lark, the narrator, who dreamed of being an explorer from boyhood, takes on his first assignment. He lands a job that promises to bring excitement, if not glamour. It turns out to be quite an internship for him. Marlow embarks on a journey that will take him not only up the Congo but into the realm of human experience, where the age-old struggle between good intentions and the human lust for power and loot is central. The youthful traveler identifies with the enigmatic figure by the name of Kurtz. The evolving image of the master ivory collector and superior force embodied in Kurtz serves as the lodestar for Marlow's navigation up the river to its source. Kurtz becomes a forerunner of Marlow and stands as a haunting symbol of human potential gone wrong. The book invites us to penetrate "the heart of darkness," an image pointing to the jungles of Africa and the interior of man.

Through this experience among other people and in a different land, we, like Marlow, learn about ourselves and our moral bearings, what constitutes savagery and how it can overtake our frailly civilized selves. The book deliberately traces a route of trade and an attitude of mind. We see undeveloped countries turned into colonies and exploited by the world powers of the late 19th century. Africa was carved into pieces and taken over by the Belgians, the British, the French, and other European nations. We come to question the mix of motives for the presence of the Europeans in the Dark Continent. Kurtz identified with the ideals of "the white man's burden." But his high hopes gradually erode. He succumbs to primitive passions. Ultimately, he bares his soul and confesses to "his own exalted and incredible degradation" (61)—his descent into the lower regions of human behavior. As Conrad, in jaundiced irony, comments, "The mind of man is capable of anything" (32). This tale probes the awful ambiguity of humans reaching beyond the ordinary. It reveals the latent savagery in so-called enlightened and civilized nations and their citizens abroad on a mission that runs afoul and turns dubious. The lesson learned is that evil is not out there but in here.

The rationalization of motives underlying relations between undeveloped and progressive countries, how thin the separation between barbarism and civilization, and the mystifying dichotomy of darkness and light or ignorance and knowledge—Conrad explores these themes from an ironic stance. Replace ivory with oil and the Congo with the Middle East, or consider coffee and South America, and the story instantly becomes as contemporary as today's newspapers and televised newscasts. The book raises questions about the policies and practices of the world's superpowers with respect to other nations. As a point of fact, under the rule of Leopold II of Belgium, in the 1880s and 90s, the Congo Free State experienced unspeakable atrocities. Political rhetoric and missionary zeal covered the exploitation of natives as enslaved people and the wholesale removal of natural resources (first ivory and then rubber). Conrad winces as he contemplates the mixed messages of the imperialist powers. His surrogate, Marlow, sarcastically exposes the discrepancy between the stated public policy and the real motive of one country's involvement in the affairs of another country. He stares into the soul of humanity and sees its terrible potential. That's the vision presented in *Heart of Darkness*. Caught up in the journey to and conquest of the lands that belong to others, the invader becomes the savage and is subject to "all that mysterious life of the wilderness that stirs in the forest, in the jungles, in the hearts of wild men," and succumbs to "The fascination of the abomination" (4).

Conrad's way of telling his tale of travel into the interior of Africa involves a frame, just as do many other tales of travel—*The Rime of the Ancient Mariner* or *The Canterbury Tales*, for instance. Marlow's fellow crew members on the sailboat, whom to stress their universality Conrad identifies by professions but keeps nameless, and their point of origin, London, are chosen to widen the setting and accountability of the tale. Another device of the telling is how the narrator unfolds Kurtz's identity. Only as the narrator learned of Kurtz, through the bits and pieces he picked up along the way from reliable and unreliable sources, is the reader, the audience addressed, allowed to make out the picture emerging. It is like looking at an impressionist painting. Too close, the canvas appears to be simply smears and dots of paint; further back, the verisimilitude comes into focus, and the fragments cohere. At one point, which proves a crucial epiphany, Marlow engages the reader in an exercise of straining to see details and discover their import. He peers through his telescope to get closer to the compound belonging to Kurtz. The posts are capped—not architecturally as his first glimpse suggests, but, as the lens permits closer inspection—with shrunken heads, impaled as threats to any who might contravene the wishes and demands of the god or demon whom Kurtz incarnated. For the uninitiated and veteran non-native alike, the jungle itself, thickly forested and shaded, full of dangers and challenges, and echoing with incomprehensible drum beats and sounds of wild animals, obscures the vision and compounds the difficulty of understanding its mysteries. It remains as unknowable as the inner recesses of the human heart.

In his voyage up the Congo, "traveling back to the earliest beginnings of the world" (30), Marlow is increasingly compelled onward by the "mystery" of Kurtz. In meeting and pondering the complex figure of Kurtz, Marlow discovers truths about himself and humankind. He becomes Kurtz's self-appointed executor: "I was to have the care of his memory" (46). He carries back the story of Kurtz, but in assessing and judging what Kurtz was and what he became, he must modify the truth to capture and articulate that legacy. His admiration of Kurtz is based both on the superiority of the man as the preeminently civilized, artistic, and well-intentioned person and "emissary of light" (10) that he was at the outset as well as on the fallen creature whom he had become as acknowledged in his deathbed utterance: "The horror! The horror!" Marlow, who detests falsehood, is forced into making a judgment in the face of a dilemma, simultaneously recognizing in Kurtz both the noble intent of the venture at the outset and his subsequent moral decline, the collapse of restraint, and surrender to the demonic. Marlow rationalizes the persistent conquest of the weak by the strong. "What redeems it," he claims, "is the idea only" (4). Marlow refuses to discard the initial Kurtz, the Kurtz before the fall, having witnessed Kurtz's deathbed admission of his "horror," his final vision of the heart of darkness in the dim light. Marlow's foil, Kurtz, is the embodiment and potentiality of each individual, including, as Marlow perceives, himself. To protect the reputation of a "universal genius" (67) gone mad, before surrendering the treatise Kurtz had written on the methods for enlightening the savages, Marlow removes the offensive words, "'Exterminate all the brutes!'" (46), which Kurtz had added as a defiant postscript. Marlow chooses to preserve the truth at the root of Kurtz's "remarkable" nature. His white lie to the Intended ironically serves to honor the Kurtz she knew. Marlow declares near the end of his journey that he "did not betray Mr. Kurtz" but remained true or "loyal to the nightmare of his choice" (59).

Repeatedly in telling his tale, Marlow likens his experience to a bad dream. The nightmarish landscape intensifies the absurdity of the characters he encounters. From the bizarre women in black occupied in knitting and the doctor with his calibers measuring the skulls of the new employees to the black men in chains, who in the throes of death look contorted like "bundles of acute angles" (14), to the Russian dressed in motley and the decorated female savage—the gallery of portraits is phantasmagoric. The tale of the demise of Marlow's predecessor, Fresleven, is ominous. The utter futility of the enterprise as embodied in the bricklayer who stays idle and symbolized by the upside-down railway car and later the stockpile of ivory at the inner station contribute to the tale's dream motif. Conrad's figurative and allusive language enlarges the story's scale. Primary is the light-and-dark, white-and-black imagery, beginning with reference to dominos on board the sailboat and culminating in the human skulls and elephant tusks that betoken the ravaging of life and resources by foreign greed and force.

Not a mere guide to parts of Africa, Conrad's tale is hypnotic in its deliberately wayward course to the source of the river Congo, to the interior load of ivory, and ultimately to the theatre of human subjugation of an indigenous people for profit and perverse mastery. The tale depicts, as does the film *Apocalypse Now*, taking the novel turned movie script and the Vietnam War as its starting point, a nightmare reality. Reading the novel, we see inner darkness from the shadows of a thickly sequestered jungle, a setting that offers a haunting symbol of the human heart.

A GUIDE TO *ON THE ROAD*

Jack Kerouac's account of an epic set of trips across the United States of the late 40s and early 50s, *On the Road*, published in 1957, is both a period piece and a work of universal appeal. Regarded as the Bible of the Beat Generation, the book portrays the lifestyle of the Beats, precursors of the Hippies and practitioners of a fast-moving, devil-may-care attitude, elevated by drugs and alcohol to flights of fancy. It serves as a singular documentary of a generation of young people who chose to drift and careen at high speed. On the road, they travel by car, bus, or truck (as a passenger, driver, owner, hitchhiker, or paid transporter). They are intent on hooking some mileage on a train or in a car or, alternatively, parked in a chair or lounging on a bed. One conspicuous aspect of the portrait of the beats is the use of authentic slang. Kerouac draws on the era's lingo in his coming of age semi-autobiographical novel. To express admiration, the cult he depicts in his characters is given to the then-current words such as "mad," "gun," "beat," "gone," "balling," and "dig."

On the Road is a madcap journey back and forth across the continent. Departing from urban New York and racing to reach Denver and the surrounding high peaks of the Rockies, the itinerants, after a brief but intense salute to high living there, floor it on to California, San Francisco, and the blue Pacific. Getting their fill of bouts of pleasure in the West, they catapult into the interior of Mexico. Throughout the travels, the narrator keeps company with numerous partners from a largely nomadic cult. At every turn, Kerouac amplifies the excitement by sustaining a mood of anticipation—of getting West and to particular cities, towns, the mountains, and other landmark places. And, at the same time, of getting drunk and partying, having sex, and meeting others who share their beathood. Even if it's the frantic hope of finishing a manuscript or simply stopping to have a bite to eat, especially apple pie and ice cream, an attitude of fervor prevails. The dominant desire is, of course, to hit the road or jump a freight train if the opportunity is there. But highest in the gamut of priorities for Kerouac is that of gaining truth.

In a breathless moment, the thrill of approaching the Pacific Ocean is captured in celebrative words: "We . . . saw . . . ahead of us the fabulous white city of San Francisco on her eleven mystic hills with the blue Pacific and its advancing wall of potato-patch fog beyond, and smoke and goldenness in the late afternoon of time" (158). Sal—the name the author bestows on his narrator—has an unquenchable case of wanderlust, remaining strong after the initial trip west and far from jaded upon repeated returns to all points west.

The characters are deftly penned, the salient features and memorable habits of each preserved as if by the scissored hand of a silhouette cutter on the sidewalks of Paris. The narrator himself, Sal Paradise, and his hero, Dean Moriarty, walk away with the prize. But Marylou, Camille, Sal's aunt, Carlo Marx, Chad King, Tim Gray, Remi Boncoeeur and his girlfriend Lee Ann, Ed and Galatea Dunkel, Ray Rawlins and his sister Babe, Eddie, Old Bull Lee and his bitter but devoted wife Jane, Roland Major, Terry and her brother Rickey, Ed Wall and his family, whose ranch the gang visits, Stan Shephard, Slim Gaillard, Little Alfred, and Laura—the cast is phenomenal. Each is idiosyncratically portrayed, and all contribute to the group picture, both the verbal photos taken on the road and the memorable snapshots in the album of visits and parties along the way. Terry's brother, for example, comes to life with his carousing and pet phrase, "Dah you go—dah you go, man!" Whether it is "the Ghost of the Susquehanna" or any of the many characters they pick up on the way, each occupies a place in the fast-moving gallery of portraits.

The dialogue is excellent. Chapter 4, Part One, is worth reading again and again. The ride on a flatbed truck driven by farm boys from Minnesota stands out as a tour de force. It is a stand-up piece—literally—for Sal and the others who hold on for dear life, nearly tossed off the platform when attempting to relieve themselves, a necessity made more urgent, given the volume of alcohol being consumed on board. The antics are a source of uncontrolled amusement for the young driver and his in-cab passenger, who are on leave from the sobering chores of the farm back home. It is fun to observe the author's use of epithets (apt shortcuts to characterization as memorialized by Dickens in *Pickwick Papers*) and his portraiture of the microcosm clinging to the swerving, speeding truck headed for L.A.

Time and again, Kerouac references the firmament and vast vistas. Substituting for Homer's "rosy-fingered dawn," Kerouac's epic formula, colorfully varied throughout the text, has the sun rhythmically turning the landscape red or purple as dusk settles in. The perspective of the sky, its immensity and mystery, is often enlarged to dwarf the company of travelers on the road below or to guide them onward and upward. "We zoomed through another crossroads town, . . . and returned to the tremendous darkness, and the stars overhead were pure and bright because of the increasingly thin air as we mounted the high hill of the western plateau" (25-26). Denver is enchanted and "holy"; "Carlo and I went through rickety streets in the Denver night. The air was soft, the stars so fine, the promise of every cobbled alley so great, that I thought I was in a dream" (38). The stellar scene above casts a melancholy glow on events depicted as bittersweet by the narrator: "Dust rose to the stars together with every sad music on earth" (205). Kerouac finds satisfaction in the continuity of the elements overhead, noting that "At night in this part of the West the stars, as I had seen them in Wyoming, are big as roman candles and as lonely as the Prince of the Dharma who's lost his ancestral grove and journeys across the spaces between points in the handle of the Big Dipper, trying to find it again" (211). The descriptions of the night sky and the stars and the ancient constellations they form contribute not simply a sense of navigation but a spirit of awe. They are the nocturnal canopy of the book and reflect a round-the-clock quest on the road below for a mysterious, longed-for destination. They, as much as the odometer, speak to the distances yet to travel. The stated goal of the narrator is "to pursue my star further" (52).

The places flash by as more than points on a compass or dots on a map. They are preludes to further excitement. "It was getting better as I got deeper into Iowa, the pie bigger, the ice cream richer. There were the most beautiful bevies of girls everywhere I looked in Des Moines that afternoon" (14). However, the hedonists sort out their potential pleasures and discipline themselves to postpone for later fulfillment. Sal passes up pursuit of the immediate satisfaction for the more distant, accepting the hitchhiking and bussing ahead more readily because of the promise of "a ball in Denver. Carlo Marx was already in Denver; Dean was there; Chad King and Tim Gray were there, it was their hometown; Marylou was there; and there was mention of a mighty gang including Ray Rawlins and his beautiful blond sister Babe Rawlins; two waitresses Dean knew, the Bettencourt sisters, and even Roland Major, my old college writing buddy, was there. I looked forward to all of them with joy and anticipation. So I rushed past the pretty girls, and the prettiest girls in the world live in Des Moines" (14). Dean and the gang that gathers around him seldom forgo—but, in fact, by plan or whim, create their own—sybaritic holidays, all-night binges of booze, drugs, rambling conversations, and sex. En route to Mexico City, Sal, Dean, and Stan, tearing through the desert heat, make a stop in Gregoria, where they get high and, guided by Victor, a guy they've picked up on the road, spend money and time in a whorehouse, putting on a spectacle for the locals. For participants and readers alike, it is an unforgettable experience that Sal alludes to when sobered up as "a pornographic hasheesh daydream in heaven" (277).

Pleasure comes from living fast and traveling at high speed. One sweep across the land deserves another. One of the numerous vehicles pressed into service to traverse the continent, a Cadillac being trolleyed at breakneck velocity for its absentee owner, hurls Dean—arms draped over the steering wheel and talking a blue streak—and Sal and their paying passengers across the country. The speedometer breaks at 110. Detailed and accelerated too are a slew of other vehicles put to the long-distance, top-speed test: the team-driven travel-bureau cars, Dean's '49 Hudson and, later, his '37 Ford Sedan, and those vehicles Sal alone or with his buddies, male and female alike, hook rides in when not catching a boxcar, settling for a bus when thumbing it isn't doing the trick, or stealing a car, in the dark of night, when pressing on seems important and the chances of getting caught are less risky. Dean is in his element when coasting the car at perilous speeds, not solely to save gas but to intensify the thrill, down the mountainous hairpin curves to reach the San Joaquin Valley.

Out of Omaha, where Sal catches sight of his first cowboy, he and a hitchhiker friend take up an offer to help out by driving one of a cowboy's two cars a hundred miles west. A deal! They "ball[ed] that jack ninety miles an hour out of sheer exuberance" (16). In such fashion—begging, borrowing, stealing—they hopscotch their way West, enjoying every moment and mile of the way. A sense of the West is pervasive and distinctive.

At a diner, they encounter the West personified.

> I heard a great laugh, the greatest laugh in the world, and here came this rawhide old-timer Nebraska farmer with a bunch of other boys into the diner; you could hear his raspy cries clear across the plains, across the whole gray world of them that day. Everybody else laughed with him. He didn't have a care in the world and had the hugest regard for everybody. I said to myself, Wham, listen to that man laugh. That's the West, here I am in the West. . . . And he threw himself on a stool and went hyaw hyaw hyaw hyaw. . . . It was the spirit of the West sitting right next to me. (17)

Elsewhere exuberant laughs punctuate episodes of fun. Joyful laughter accompanies Dean's ebullient monologues. The laugh of the Minnesota farm boys is unforgettable. Remi's "tremendous laugh roared over the California woods and over America" (65). It erupts first when Remi catches sight of Sal wiggling through a small window to enter the bedroom where he and Lee Ann, his bitter but devoted girlfriend, are sleeping. Remi repeatedly explodes in guffaws when he gleefully goes over and over the incident of Sal's hilarious forced entry. Coincidentally, his neighbor Mr. White's laugh is said to eclipse Remi's in robustness, hyperbolically declared "the one greatest laugh in all this world" (56). Yet it is hard to match the riotous peals from Old Bill Lee, whose enlightening conversations, drawing from his worldwide travel, voracious reading, comprehensive experience, devotion to experimentation, and preference for earlier times, are heightened by every drug in the book. When Sal and his friends descend upon him in New Orleans, in an interlude marked by novelty and outrageous hospitality, they witness his and his wife's round-the-clock fixes and Old Bill's ready tongue. Throughout the book, laughter splashes against the waves of sad introspection that intermittently overcome Sal, who is predisposed from time to time to be critical of the lives and times he and his friends are living with abandon and via a plethora of stimulants. While in the Mississippi delta, Sal speaks of his gang as "members of our sad drama in the American night" and alludes to the certainty that "dark laughter would come again" (138).

The arrival in Denver is, of course, a high point. In the last stretch, "I tingled all over; I counted minutes and subtracted miles" (32). Sal fantasizes as he approaches: "I pictured myself in a Denver bar that night, with all the gang, and in their eyes I would be strange and ragged and like the Prophet who has walked across the land to bring the dark Word, and the only Word I had was 'Wow!'" Let off at Larimer Street, he "stumbled along with the most wicked grin of joy in the world, among the old bums and beat cowboys of Larimer Street" (32). There in Denver, the party explodes. It erupts again in San Francisco. And it bangs all along the road in between. For Sal and the gang, "The road is life" (200).

The saga sours, however, as Sal's respect for Dean becomes a memory and the heroic Dean evaporates as a present phenomenon. In Sal's "vision," Dean remains quintessentially the "con-man" and "HOLY GOOF," an "angel" too far gone, "too mad." Sal delivers the verdict on him midway in the novel: "He giggled maniacally and didn't care" (145). Dean's abandonment of his friend, which occurs in Mexico, the breakup of Dean's own family, and the collapse of their pipe dream to band together in New York and return to California before embarking for Italy—the decline takes its toll on the spirit of hope and satisfaction. In the end, Sal is left only the laurels of legend to brood upon in solitary reflection and wonder, the experiences on the road now over.

NAIPAUL'S ISLAMIC JOURNEY

V. S. Naipaul's *Among the Believers: An Islamic Journey*, published in 1981, is an account of seven months of travel and life among the peoples of Iran, Pakistan, Malaysia, and Indonesia, in 1979. The author's purpose was to become acquainted with and assess the Islamic faith as incarnated in those he met and as reflected in the results of the activities of countless others. He discovered that the believers cling to their religion with unbending obedience and dogged determination to take over the world. His journey reveals both the riddle and contradictions of Islam. Muslim belief, as portrayed by Naipaul, defies reason and is anachronistic. The juxtaposition of technology and the backward orientation of the faith makes for an enigma. As the title implies, the focus is on delineating the beliefs shared by a group, a close-up revelation of the insiders' views and doctrines, and the variations of that theme as witnessed in different non-Arab lands. At the same time, the title suggests the location of an outsider traveling "among" those in residence, reporting what he finds out about their faith and convictions. The subtitle and the designated places visited announce the large borders within which the excursion is taken.

In 1998, *Beyond Belief: Islamic Excursions Among the Converted Peoples*, a sequel to *Among the Believers*, appeared. In it, Naipaul recounts his travels to the same territories during a half year in 1995. He already explored the roots of his ancestry in India and the Hinduism of his family in *An Area of Darkness* (1964), *The Overcrowded Barracoon* (1972), and *India: A Wounded Civilization* (1977). Later, in 1990, he returned to the subject in *India: A Million Mutinies Now*.

Prompted by televised news reports on the Iranian revolution and by a novel he read about Iran, wanting to understand the origin and extent of Muslims' deep passion and fanaticism, Naipaul went to Iran and neighboring countries to see for himself what made Islam tick. He uncovers a "religion of fear and reward, oddly compounded with war and worldly grief" (12). In this respect, he is struck by the partial resemblance to Christianity.

Islam in thought and action pivots on a tenacious acceptance of the authority of its historical revelation and dogma in the person of the Prophet and the *Koran*, in which sacred texts and the pronouncements of subsequent holy men of Mecca call for rigid adherence to its laws. The five daily prayers define the routine and devotion of its adherents. All else pales; everything else is set aside. For those moments, Muslims are called to pray. The ritual is paramount. From dawn to sunset on the holy days of Ramadan, devout Muslims fast and pray, first engaging in a ceremonial washing and cleaning of their bodies. White turbans, black-cloaked figures, and veiled women paint a picture of the past laminated to the present.

In the nooks and crannies explored on his journey, Naipaul meets an array of interesting people. One is a lawyer who shows him a stupendous library. Another is a learned man who lectures Naipaul on an obscure Arab philosopher from the 10th century. A doctor's son he meets has read hundreds of English novels. He comes across teachers, poets, government officials, and scores of ordinary and exceptional people. Getting acquainted with a variety of residents helps him tell the story and, in the process, weave a colorful and rare tapestry defining motifs distinctive to Islam. Parts of the book read like a catechism, or colloquy, recounting interviews and resembling high-level journalism and good fiction in the same breath.

Among the Believes, blending the topical and the universal or cyclical is a search for the continuing and expansive appeal of Islam, a way of life that insists on strict discipline and demarks behavioral boundaries between and for males and females. The followers of Islam, in the main, are not ecumenical; their way is exclusive. They strive to have their religion monopolize and prevail, turning to it as the sole guide to political and personal life. Ideally, Islam is a formation rendered in a sort of theocracy, a community led by chosen leaders who embody the teachings, mystique, and zeal requisite to overcoming all other rival and existing modes of political and religious expression. Naipaul makes the point that, while in some ways akin to revolutionary socialism or communism, the notable difference being the upholding by Islam of the conviction that there is a hereafter, Islam disparages any other forms of governance.

A large share of the perceived fascination over the hold that the Muslim religion has on its adherents rests on the odd juxtaposition and tug-of-war between a retreat to past revelation, dogma, and pronouncements for a life of restraint and prescribed behaviors and an acquiescence to the infrastructure and amenities beholden to technology. The West is anathema, and yet many of its trappings are countenanced. Among the believers, he witnesses lots of bashing of Western ways. In their estimation, the liberal penchant flaunted in America is particularly targeted. The believers he meets, representative of millions more, uncritically laud Islamic rules and discipline. Most of the devout people Naipaul encounters open up to him, though they see him as an outsider. He is not regarded as an infidel, perhaps because he has the license of a writer and genuine inquirer.

From the travels of Naipaul, Islam in thought and action emerges as a regressive belief. On what persistent authenticity among the hordes of its followers does it pivot? Their unwavering acceptance of the authority of its historical revelation and dogma through the Prophet and later caliphs and their rigid adherence to its laws. Their laws are many and—as outsiders would regard—exceedingly invasive and burdensome. The believer surrenders all in unquestioned faith. The true Muslim accepts and demands a way of life that tolerates no deviation from authority, all in the name of Allah. It is blind faith that seeks all the answers in the *Koran*. Naipaul, speaking of the fanatical aspect of the religion, comments: "The open-and-shut morality of Islam, always with its answers in the book or in the doings of the Prophet" (353). In "Islamization," he notes a "stupefaction, greater than any that could have come with a Western-style curriculum" (325).

An aspect of Islam present in the lands Naipaul visits is a dominant note of anachronism. The study of Arabic by Muslims beyond Mecca, their travel there as pilgrims, and the dress codes all hark back to the formative period of Islam. In *Beyond Belief*, Naipaul again addresses the phenomenon of converts: "Islam is in its origins an Arab religion.

Everyone not an Arab who is a Muslim is a convert. Islam is not simply a matter of conscience or private belief. It makes imperial demands. A convert's worldview alters. His holy places are in Arab lands; his sacred language is Arabic. His idea of history alters. He rejects his own; he becomes, whether he likes it or not, a part of the Arab story." Naipaul presses the point of the clash of orientations, declaring that "in the Islam of converted countries there is an element of neurosis and nihilism." Indeed, he observes, "These countries can be easily set on the boil" ([xi]).

There is, especially in Indonesia, a sort of eclecticism, an incorporation of rituals, ideas, and customs pervasive in the religion that preceded the arrival of Islam. This feature of Islam is analogous to how Catholicism, when transported to the New World, picked up remnants of the former and ongoing beliefs and practices of the natives undergoing conversion.

As in other tales of travel, in Naipaul's book, the reader not only learns about local customs and meets interesting people but also finds out about the climates, landmarks, vegetation, and features peculiar to the places visited. From the swirl of pedestrian and vehicular traffic in Tehran, he boards for the hundred-mile train ride south to the holy city of Qom. He shares the trip with Behzad and his girlfriend, two chatterbox, card-playing-till-caught, hopeful revolutionaries. From there, he catches a flight over fields and mountains to Mashhad, five hundred miles northeast of Tehran and close to the borders of Russia and Afghanistan. On the return rail trip, Naipaul traverses Iran. In Pakistan, Malaysia, and Indonesia, he visits numerous cities (most of them smog-ridden and densely populated), schools, mosques, museums, and out-of-the-way places. His itinerary stretches from Jakarta to the Himalayas, covering a vast expanse of lands and seething masses of humanity. His journey on the micro-level is subject to impromptu meetings, changes in appointed meetings, and exigencies and hassles involving airport schedules, searches, and delays. It is a tale that elicits interest on multiple levels, not only as an encyclopedic quest for the identity of Islam.

The persons whom he meets stand out as in an album. Some whom he depicts in detail appear to be characters from the pages of a novel. His chosen interpreter and guide in Iran is a young man named Behzad, a non-believer like Naipaul. After a futile trip to the bus station and a taxi ride back to the city's core, the pair gingerly dodge traffic as they tramp back and forth to the hotel. The driving practices of urban Iranians, as attested to by their dented cars and bicycles and the woeful statistics of casualties, make travel precarious. But as we learn, Naipaul was, literally, in good hands. For Behzad, when he had zigzagged across an intersection and made it through, looking back to see his timid companion stranded on the other side, returned to assist his friend. "He led me by the hand; and, just as the moorhen places herself a little downstream from the chick, breaking the force of the current which would otherwise sweep the little thing away forever, so Behzad kept me in his lee, walking a little ahead of me and a little to one side, so that he would have been hit first" (6). In this and other situations, the narrator is frequently befriended and accorded hospitality and given a lot or at least significant fragments of relevant background information for the journey. At times when he doesn't gain much knowledge from an interlocutor, as in the case of Khalkhalli, "Khomeini's hanging judge" (37), the ayatollah whom Naipaul is granted an audience with in Qom, he settles for opportunities as concessions to gauge human oddities. With Khalkhalli, he confronts a person proud of having a hand in the history of executions and still celebrating his gun. Other times he meets editors, poets, and teachers who add colorful strokes to the canvas he is painting.

The descriptions of landscapes and architecture embellish the travelogue and keep the countries visited from becoming a blur. Looking out the windows of a train, Naipaul sees the countryside—"a landscape of mountains, hills, and irrigated plain"—flow by. "The fields were golden, after the harvest; and in the late afternoon the distant hills became warm brown. The land was dug up here and there by watercourses, which . . . now, in the height of summer . . . had dwindled to rippled rivulets a couple of feet wide and a few inches deep. Flocks of lambs fed on the stubble. Sometimes men could be seen winnowing. But the modern road was never far away, and the brilliantly coloured trucks; and power pylons marched across the plain." He continues, "The villages were the colour of mud; and the houses had domed clay roofs (timber for beams not being easy to come by here), with slanting pipes at the bottom to drain the water off" (74).

The chapter title "Karachi Phantasmagoria" captures the multifaceted panoply of the country set aside expressly for India's Muslim population, separating it from the multitudinous Hindu population of India. In contrast, a stopover in the foothills of the Himalayas turns into a highlight when Naipaul and his companion Masood are invited to share in the life and meal of a nomadic family, whose sheep and goats were allowed to enter and leave the tent quarters at will. Other livestock—camels, cattle, ponies, and donkeys—were either tethered or free to range nearby or, at times, wander into the tent to raid the hay stashed inside for the sheep. There and farther up in the mountains, as they climb the heights by jeep, they enter a peaceable and seemingly timeless kingdom.

The tale of Naipaul's sojourn among the populous Islam nations beyond the Arab birthplace of their faith is a kaleidoscope. While each country's character stands out silhouetted against the others, the shards of their different colors coalesce to evoke a momentary prismatic image. Each is a distinctive piece in the puzzle that makes up the Muslim religion. Each territory has evolved its strain of the faith, and its peoples, cities, and customs contribute to the mosaic. The reader is swept along as on a river, gazing at the shorelines that vary but always mark the course of the same current. The stream is a powerful force, permanently changing the contours of the land and its inhabitants in surrender to Allah.

COLERIDGE'S *RIME OF THE ANCIENT MARINER*

Homer's *Odyssey*, Chaucer's *Canterbury Tales*, the medieval morality play *Everyman*, Bunyan's *Pilgrim's Progress*, Swift's *Gulliver's Travels*, Defoe's *Robinson Crusoe*, Twain's *Huck Finn*—such works relate the events of wayfaring, be it by a voyage, a trip, a journey, or a pilgrimage. They are tales of travel. So too is Coleridge's narrative poem *The Rime of the Ancient Mariner*. The skeleton or framework of the narrative is a voyage. It serves as a clothesline on which the garments and events hang in the breeze.

The Rime of the Ancient Mariner owes a lot to the many accounts of discoveries and explorations that the poet Coleridge had apparently read about or was familiar with. As we call to mind recorded voyages, and sea-way passages, the name Columbus soars to the forefront. Navigators such as Marco Polo, Vasco de Gama, Magellan, Sir Francis Drake, and Capt. James Cook stand out for their explorations and spirit of adventure. Sailing charted and uncharted seas, they set out in search of new directions to connect continents, establish speedier trade routes, and claim land for their patrons. With the history of circumnavigations of the globe, we find ourselves looking ahead to the construction of the Panama Canal. This event radically changed the course of sailing between the oceans.

The twofold pattern of exploration by sea is familiar: the voyages are to the known and the unknown; they venture out and may make it back. In the *Ancient Mariner*, we travel that vast sweeping curve or loop experienced by captains of old. The "Argument" or statement that heads the poem reads like a mariner's log: "How a ship, having first sailed to the Equator, was driven by storms to the cold Country towards the South Pole; how the Ancient Mariner cruelly and in contempt of the laws of hospitality killed a Seabird and how he was followed by many and strange judgments: and in what manner he came back to his own Country." Even more explicitly and in detail, the account is recorded in the "Gloss" or running commentary in the left margin, which provides a way to preview and interpret the story.

The voyage's grand structural line provides the poem's basic outline. We can readily follow its itinerary, noting how Coleridge plotted (or charted) its course. Starting with stanza 6, in enchanting ballad lines, predominantly penned in quatrains, we read of the setting forth, the embarking:

> The ship was cheered, the harbor cleared,
> Merrily did drop
> Below the kirk, below the hill,
> Below the lighthouse top (ll.21-24).

The familiar landscape is left behind. From now till the end, we are awash in a seascape. In the next stanza, we note from the directions that the ship is sailing southward, for "The Sun came up upon the left." Stanza 8 details more progress. We can construct the first lap of the voyage based on the fact that the sun is above the ship's mast: the ship has reached the Equator. In stanza 11, storm winds drive the ship south to the South Pole, where the mariner and his crew arrive at the dangerous, frigid Cape Horn, with its "snowy cliffs" and huge crackling icebergs—all depicted in rhythmic lines of visual and auditory imagery. "The ice was here, the ice was there, / The ice was all around: / It cracked and growled, and roared and howled" (ll. 59-61).

After the men experience the terrors of the polar ice, an Albatross appears. Its company is brief, however, for inexplicably, it is shot by the Mariner. His deed is "a hellish thing," as the Mariner admits. The act appears to have deprived the mariners of the breeze powering their ship. All had been progressing till then. From the first stanza of Part II, we learn that they've rounded Cape Horn and are heading north into the Pacific, for "the Sun now rose upon the right." When the crucial cape had been navigated, the next stage of the voyage would be the long northwesterly run before the trade winds toward the Line (that is, the Equator). In stanza 5, the narrator reports, in a burst of fricatives and voiced stops:

> The fair breeze blew, the white foam flew,
> The furrow followed free;
> We were the first that ever burst
> Into that silent sea.

The poet has caught, and the reader feels, the thrill experienced by all the discoverers and their league who have sailed those seas. The puffing of alliterative fricatives animates the auspicious winds and the wake they produce. Then, with the abruptness like that of the fall of the shot bird off the Cape, the ship is at the Line: "Down dropped the breeze, the sails dropped down" (l. 07). When the ship reaches the Equator, the voyage as a structural pattern in the poem ends. Near the close of Part V, the ship is still at the Equator. With the calms of the Line left behind, the voyage from the Equator to the Equator round the Horn has been fulfilled.

Among the strange events that ensue are the visit by Death and Life-in-Death, whose casting of dice results in the death, "one by one," of the entire crew. As punishment, the lone Mariner is forced to witness his men's souls departing and must abide their cursing looks for "Seven days, seven nights." Out of the realm of the known—once the Mariner is overcome by a deep reverence for nature's bountiful creatures—the ship miraculously resumes its course. When the mariner awakens from his trance, he beholds his native country. The travels of the Ancient Mariner involve a voyage "out" and a voyage "back"—different forces at work in each portion. The winds on the voyage derive from nature, but those guiding the ship homeward are beholden to spiritual powers beyond human understanding or contrivance. By supernatural powers, the soulless men are resuscitated to assist in navigating back to home port before disappearing.

The poem is a frame story. Its meaning is embedded in how the story is told and revealed in the events that make up the tale. The narrator's intermittent pauses intensify his hold on his listener, the wedding guest whom he has accosted. Assured of his listener's attention, he resumes telling his adventurous tale as if compelled to share and dwell on the lesson it taught him. The frame in which the picture is placed, the dramatic framework of the account, is the story's completion. The occasional interruptions by the wedding guest during the Mariner's telling of his experience at sea reifies the tension between engagement in the flow of ordinary human events and apprehension at contemplating deeply spiritual and troubling matters. The listener, alarmed at what he is hearing and put off by the aggressive mien of the narrator, expresses his desire and the urgency as "next of kin" to join the wedding party festivities at the kirk, but, like others to come, is held captive by the grim tale and grip of the Ancient Mariner. The intrusions highlight the need for humankind to attend to sobering moral truths, acknowledge their preeminence even amid the merry life removed from and oblivious to the toll of death, and heed the call to forgiveness and salvation. The moments of interaction between the spinner of the yarn and his captive audience provide a contrast between two aspects of reality. The effect of the interruptions and colloquy is to document that two kinds of reality—two hemispheres of existence, the mundane and the spiritual, the understood and the mysterious—are ever-present and interconnected.

The Mariner's tale is a confession. He harms an innocent creature and comes to feel guilt and remorse. When he eventually blesses and celebrates the beauty of the sea creatures, resplendent in the moonlit water, the spell on the journey is broken. His compassion for nature and other living creatures is a sign of recovered love and an indicator of his progress toward salvation. The loss of the albatross around his neck and its dropping into the sea is emblematic of his acknowledgment of guilt and the beginning of forgiveness. Rain descends to quench the Mariner's physical thirst. He is granted the refreshment of sleep, the skeleton crew is resuscitated, and empowering winds arise to hasten the craft to its destination. As the gloss puts it, "The curse is finally expiated." What remains for the Mariner on his return to land and upon the shriving by the Hermit is to seek out penance: his task, the price he has to pay for his misdeed which estranged him from grace, is to wander and tell those he encounters the story of his voyage and its outcome.

> I pass, like night, from land to land;
> I have strange power of speech;

That moment that his face I see,
I know that man that must hear me:
To him my tale I teach. . . .
He prayeth well, who loveth well
Both man and bird and beast.

The returned traveler and those to whom he tells his tale of travel are "sadder . . . and wiser." Not solely the person who journeys but also those who experience the journey vicariously through their reading or hearing of it gain expanded knowledge from experience shared. Some readers believe that the Mariner is reinstated in society at the end of the poem. Others see him as an outcast, one condemned to wander. The theme of isolation looms large in the work, both when the Mariner is at sea and later when he is back on land. At sea, he is "Alone, alone, all, all alone, / Alone on a wide wide sea! / And never a saint took pity on / My soul in agony." Returned to his homeland, a solitary figure, he journeys from community to community, no longer accorded permanent residency and participation in the community of his origin. The setting, both at sea and on shore, becomes symbolic. While pronounced differently than, say, in *Pilgrim's Progress*, where allegory is omnipresent, the physical imagery and the actions of the traveler likewise, in *Rime*, convey spiritual states. For the Mariner, evil and disaster mostly occur in the sunlight while phases of redemption unfold under the light of the moon. As in Conrad's *Heart of Darkness*, so in *The Rime of the Ancient Mariner*, the protagonist's journey is decidedly moral. Both are tales of self-discovery and spiritual insight. The returned traveler is compelled to share his tale of discovery with others so that they too might be enlightened.

THINK AND RIDE AT THE SAME TIME

- Pirsig's *Zen and the Art of Motorcycle Maintenance* -

Robert Pirsig's *Zen and the Art of Motorcycle Maintenance*, published in 1974, is technically neither a manual for repairing and keeping up a motorcycle nor a compendium of Zen philosophy. It purports to be both an account of a motorcycle trip west and a guide to clear thinking and empirical inquiry. The author notes that the novelty of traveling by motorcycle is heightened by the fact that the vision of the world is unframed and offers more clarity than from behind a windowed vehicle. The latter "is just more TV" (4). On a cycle, a person is closer to the real world, he argues.

In the kindred spirit of travelers whose focus is the journey, Pirsig's purpose is "more to travel than to arrive anywhere" (5). Genuinely interested in seeing scenery with less disturbed enjoyment, not set on the uninterrupted speed at the cost of monotony and greater traffic, Pirsig and his traveling companions follow the side roads. That's what Pirsig defines as "mak[ing] good time" (5). It's more personal off the main highways. As he has learned, road maps are telltale: "If the line wiggles, that's good" (6). Like Frost, whose guidance he does not need to seek in this instance, Pirsig deliberately takes to the road less traveled, knowing that that makes all the difference.

Unable to maintain a lengthy conversation with a passenger or friends on the cycle ahead of theirs, the riders can, and in this case, do, take advantage of another option. As Pirsig points out, though contending with the swish of the wind, the throb of the motorcycle motor, and the alignment of the two persons seated, a traveler and partner on a motorcycle have abundant time to observe and think. Like soliloquies, Pirsig's talking aloud to the reader-cum-passenger forms what he terms "a sort of Chautauqua" (7). A distinctly American institution, the Chautauqua is what this travel book resembles: entertainment and instruction combined. For Pirsig, the questions we raise define the direction we go. He would rather ask "What is best?" than simply "What's new?" He prefers the "old channels" (8) over the new ones. The dimensions of the channel do count, however. For "There are eras of human history in which the channels of thought have been too deeply cut and no change was possible, and nothing new ever happened, and 'best' was a matter of dogma. . . . Now the stream of our common consciousness seems to be obliterating its own banks, losing its central direction and purpose, flooding the lowlands, disconnecting and isolating the highlands and to no particular purpose other than the wasteful fulfillment of its own internal momentum. Some channel deepening seems called for" (8). The passage serves as a preamble to a journey made to parallel the Chautauqua.

Ahead of the deep thinking that the book engenders, the reader is given a rundown of what the travelers have packed. Traveling on a motorcycle restricts how much can be taken along in the way of baggage. (As Simon, author of *Jupiter's Travels*, certainly knows firsthand!) Pirsig devotes several pages to detailing what he packs. The list is as Spartan as Thoreau's list of "necessaries" and excludes most of the "next to necessaries." The no-nonsense categories are Clothing, Personal Stuff, Cooking and Camping Gear, and Motorcycle Stuff. Besides the obvious—gloves and change of clothes for all weathers, canteen, compass, cooking utensils, and sleeping bags—Pirsig takes along three books: a shop manual, a trouble-shooting guide for his cycle, and—you guessed it—*Walden*. Other fundamentals include a small supply of critical tools and spare parts (spark plugs, bulbs, and the like).

En route, we are treated to the passing scenery: the prairie, the plains, the mountains, and eventually, the Pacific coast. Interlarded are details about the landscape, the trees and vegetation, the temperature, the shape of the roads, the cloud formations, the towns, the stops to grab a bite to eat or slurp down malts, and the people absorbed in their chores and activities.

The father and his son Chris are—and have—company on the trip. Their friends John and Sylvia Sutherland, who ride on the other bike, become targets for comparison. John, a musician, serves as a sounding board for the narrator; unlike his biker companion, he is not mechanical. The two men are opposites in how they approach motorcycles and view the world. For John, motors and technology are unreasonable and should be tended to by knowledgeable others and railed at when they go wrong and ignored when they work. A person adept at motors and looking at matters from the standpoint of logic and common sense, the narrator concludes that he and John reside in different "dimensions." Theirs is "a conflict of *visions of reality*" (53).

Most of the Chautauquas revolve around Phaedrus, the earlier self of the narrator. The book—"this twentieth-century odyssey of Phaedrus" (376)—is essentially a search for the identity and philosophical authenticity of Phaedrus. The narrator adopts the role of executor of Phaedrus, set on determining the nature and scope of his legacy. What gradually evolves is a story of a man who encountered a mental crisis, a crisis tied to a quest ultimately to establish the centrality of the concept of Quality and simultaneously arbitrate the tension between classical and romantic sensibilities. Pirsig is haunted by, summons as a favorite topic for Chautauquas, and tries finally to put to rest what he chooses to call "the ghost of rationality" (78).

When the narrator shifts the mindset from the Chautauqua to the actual trip, providing dialogue and detailing actions and aspects of the complicated dynamic of the father-son relationship he and Chris possess, he reverts to the present tense. The effect of the change in tense is that the reader feels more a part of the whole trip. The soliloquies do not seem so overwhelming when interludes of ongoing activity and concrete aspects of the road trip share the focus, though they are not the points of emphasis. These selfsame soliloquies become a means of marking the progress of the journey. Uniquely, the *physical* journey being delineated supports at the same time the *mental* journey being explored. The progression of thought and philosophizing yields depth to the book. The soliloquies serve as landmarks of the mental journey and assist in the reclamation of the thoughts and life of Phaedrus, the narrator's former self. The transitions between the two trips are easy and enjoyable and allow the fabric of the book to become a grand tapestry featuring the reconciliation of the present and the past and the romantic and the classical threads that snarl somewhat but ultimately weave toward a unity of purpose.

The narrator consoles himself in heavy traffic on a bad, bumpy, and patched road. "I'm just as happy to be thinking about the rational, analytical, classical world of Phaedrus," he thinks aloud. "His kind of rationality has been used since antiquity to remove oneself from the tedium and depression of one's immediate surroundings" (69), he continues. The motorcycle provides the narrator a link to explain how germane and applicable Phaedrus' logic is. The analysis of the motorcycle into its constituent parts and their respective functions makes for an enlightening mini-lecture. Later, Chautauquas amplify this starting point. Even the distinction between romantic and classical ways of regarding the world applies to the here-and-now world of the motorcycle. The differentiation between deductive and inductive reasoning likewise turns on an example from motorcycle riding and diagnosing a problem. An entire discussion defining the nature of quality is pivotal to the book's meaning. The same holds for his entertaining notion of an imaginary college course called Gumptionology 101. Going from Chicago to San Francisco, the trip is the springboard for a philosophical essay, doled out in discrete passages of golden silence as the machine roars across the landscape and measures the present time. The backdrop of ancient thought shown to be still relevant today makes for a more meditative journey than one punctuated merely by bits of ordinary conversation. The book, we could say, epitomizes Thoreau's dictum of "catch[ing] two fishes with one hook."

The beauty of Pirsig's use of the motorcycle as a doorway to understanding and care lies in his belief that "a motorcycle functions entirely in accordance with the laws of reason, and a study of the art of motorcycle maintenance is really a miniature study of the art of rationality itself" (90). It is not a case of blind faith, for he demonstrates throughout the journey that the vehicle can be cared for by exerting reason and common sense. But in addition, it takes respect, even reverence. He speaks of his tuning of his motorcycle as "a ritual" (90) and confesses that "I always feel like I'm in church when I do this" (91). He has high praise for the tools designed to work on the machine. Each one has an aesthetic ("romantic") appeal as well as a distinct ("classical") function. The trick appears to approach repairs as working on *concepts* rather than *parts*. Maintenance in the realm of technology and machinery is not as much mystery, magic, or even physical labor as it is science and logic.

The trip runs west, across the Dakotas and Montana and on to Washington state. He terms it "a kind of Northwest Passage" (99). Pirsig doesn't allow the Chautauqua to monopolize the pages of the trip's diary. The Chautauquas are significant but do not crowd out all descriptions of the landscape and weather. At one point, as they wind their way to the summit of a snow-peaked mountain, he pens a paean to mountain air and sings of the scent of pine trees, the glory of a meadow, and the thrill of seeing the thaw of winter cascading into the season of Spring. "Little streams of water run everywhere into mossy mud, and then below this into week-old grass and the small wildflowers, the tiny pink and blue and yellow and white ones which seem to pop out, sun-brilliant, from black shadows" (119). Still, the book is no epic. Nor is it Whitmanesque in the America it embraces. The Chautauqua is the principal substance of the journey. On the side trip up to the snowy top of the mountain, the narrator shifts the lens to the philosophical. "I want to talk about another kind of high country . . . the high country of the mind." Though "few people travel here" (120), the reader is a privileged invitee to the highest level of thinking. The analogy of climbing to the summit, reaching lofty heights of thought, and traversing the high country of the mind is more than a tour de force. The book's sweep of philosophic thought down through the ages is vast. Plato and Aristotle are extensively referenced, and other key philosophers—among them Hume, Locke, Kant, Hegel, Russell, Whitehead, and the earlier Greeks, Parmenides, Zeno, Heraclitus, and Thales as well as ancient Asian thinkers and their sacred texts—come into the discussion. But the chief aim of Pirsig is to assess the contribution of Phaedrus—as both the figure from the Socratic dialogue and the former self of the narrator—to the search for truth and unity and, above all, to the definition and apprehension of Quality.

The focus of the journey is philosophical. Concepts such as the nature of *a priori* knowledge and the formulation of hypotheses are to the journey here as scenery and personal encounters are to the conventional trip, to the extent that any trip is conventional. The Chautauqua is primary. At one point, the narrator apologizes for not going into depth on the characters, his companions and others whom they visit or meet on the trip, but demurs expressly, as he notes, because the book is not a novel but an unraveling of what is in and on his mind. For him, "the entire edifice of the Chautauqua" (131) gives form and meaning to the journey he recounts. Other matters seem to him more remote.

The journey, at the same time, is psychological. It is a search for Phaedrus, the past identity of the author, the admired but dimly remembered former self. When referring to his past persona, the narrator employs the third person pronoun, distorting himself from himself rather than establishing a sense of wholeness or development. Searching the past makes the narrator "feel like an archeologist." The sorting of "fragments of this memory" (139) is somewhat reminiscent of Thomas Carlyle's semi-autobiographical and philosophically oriented *Sartor Resartus.* As we travel back in time with Pirsig, we glimpse his years in India studying Eastern philosophy and flashback to his tense life as a classroom teacher at a college in Montana. Pirsig defines college, in the ideal beyond mere grades and degrees, as "the Church of Reason" (145).

Emerging from the fog are traces of his more normal phase as a father and a husband, a journalist, and an erstwhile small farmer. The period of graduate studies at the Aristotelian-bent University of Chicago is more contentious. The trip west accommodates a visit to the past with a stopover at the house of a former faculty colleague and his wife, the DeWeeses, in Bozeman, Montana. The trip in real-time and the memories it summons move the book toward completion.

The return to Montana also challenges the estrangement of the father and son, who are adjacent physically but distant psychologically. A hike up the mountain tests the strength of their relationship. They camp side-by-side in sleeping bags and ride one behind the other on the cycle, but there is a strange gap between them that pervades the journey. The son is trying to understand his father. What prevents their desired compatibility? Is it the prevailing silence of thought as they speed along? The edginess of the father at the son's reluctance to follow his instructions or share his enthusiasm for the trip? The bouts of stomach upset to which Chris is susceptible? The sense that they are marathoning a purposeless journey? Or concealed recognition by both father and son that relationships have changed, and not fully for the better?

In the end, however, the father and son experience an epiphany as they draw closer than they had been the entire trip. For traveling south on the rim of the Pacific Ocean, having removed their helmets, they enjoy seeing more clearly and hearing each other more easily, without any impairment to full sight and sound. The psychologically satisfying destination they reach without having aimed for it parallels the epiphany the narrator experiences as his Chautauqua ends on a note of fulfillment. He reaches a synthesis in his philosophical quest for unity, realizing it in his pursuit of Quality. The book circles around Quality and achieves its high point when the narrator, following the clues given by Phaedrus, discovers the essence of Quality, subservient to nothing and existing despite any attempts to define it. Without it, life is purposeless. The journey ends with that central insight and with the mutual recognition of father and son that their separation is over and that the best of the past can enhance the present and future and need not be dead and buried. Ultimately, the alleged insanity is denied, and the past is accepted as a step forward.

ADVENTURES ON THE HIGH SEAS

- Sailing the *Kon-Tiki* and *Round the World* with Captain Cook -

Two travelogues among numerous extant accounts of voyages past, most of them prosaic and not apt to prompt rereading, stand out: *The Kon-Tiki Expedition*, by Thor Heyerdahl, and Captain Cook's *Voyage Round the World*, by George Forster. While Capt. Cook's trip, one of several he is noted for, may find a reader skimming from time to time, *Kon-Tiki,* from one complete reading to the next, holds readers captive. Both works portray mariners' struggles to survive and their indomitable quest to solve a puzzle and gather firsthand information about other peoples and their places of habitation. One involves the standard sailing techniques of the late 18th century; the other attempts in the mid-20th century to replicate the primitive mode of sailing using a log-lashed raft and a single sail. Both authors record discoveries and provide lore and scientific data that other explorers have built on and revised. Central to these two accounts of a journey on the high seas is the narrator's spirit of adventure and excitement of sharing the experience day by day, episode by episode, detail upon detail.

Both Heyerdahl and Forster invoke comparisons with their use of apt similes, make references to aspects of a culture shared by the reader, and, in addition to allusions, include lines from literature and details drawn from a common education. Both travelers engage their readers and provide enjoyment and information for them throughout their respective retellings of their completed journeys.

Kon-Tiki is a wonderful adventure, with twists and turns of excitement occurring every nautical mile. At the outset, Heyerdahl articulates his theory that the Pacific islands were visited and inhabited by a race of Peruvians, Inca Indians, who 1500 years ago, long before the Spaniards landed in Peru, used balsam wood rafts to sail the 4,000-plus mile journey. Getting ready to embark takes up nearly a third of the book. First, Heyerdahl must succeed in securing financial backing. Next, he selects his crew, a variety of talented men with whom we get intimately acquainted as the voyage gets underway. On site in the jungles of Peru, the ritual of felling the perfect balsam trees and floating and hauling the logs to the shipyard for the raft construction moves the narrative forward. Each of the dozen logs is christened before it is taken down. The work was Herculean: "The ax changed hands time after time, while the splinters flew and the sweat trickled in the heat of the jungle" (53). Supplies, including a radio and basic navigational tools, World War II rations and test equipment, two-hundred coconuts, and sufficient food and water, are obtained and assigned locations aboard. The raft was built and launched on April 28, 1940; the journey for a half-dozen Scandinavians, a parrot, and a hitch-hiker hermit crab began. The saga has the men catching fish and rainwater, taking turns at maintaining the course, a regimen of two hours at the helm and three hours' rest, and, when possible, making radio contact with persons elsewhere on the globe. They frequently contend with waves and storms and, finally, with a shipwreck, going aground some distance from the planned destination. As the narrator notes, the voyage quickly "turned landlubbers into seamen" (80).

A tightly knit crew, they do not see anyone else until they reach the Pacific Islanders at the end of their trip. Heyerdahl is adept at characterization and makes each member individualized by distinguishing their manners, appearance, actions, and outlook. Their lives, their sport, and their scientific curiosity were well served by all the fish of the sea, including the flying fish that landed plentifully on the craft and didn't need to be caught or netted, and the wonderful variety of birds overhead. All creatures, including sharks, whales, and dolphins, as well as many species of fowl, become companions and not simply prey or specimens for study.

Chapters are given headings for the topics to follow, providing a sort of gloss. "Half-way" is the title of a chapter that tidily marks the halfway point both in the narrative and voyage. Throughout, the voyage and its adventures and challenges are presented in a lively manner, keeping the reader attentive as the days and nights unfold during the three months it takes to complete the trip. There is no room for tedium. Instead, every moment, every mile, is significant. The reader books passage and vicariously participates in the thrills, upsets, and ultimate success and celebration of the voyage. From the beginning point of planning to the embarkation, to the navigating and keeping body and spirit together, to the troublesome going aground at the end, readers experience the trip as if actually taken. The reader, as an armchair voyager, floats along on the raft, joins one or two of the stalwart mariners when they are out in the rubber boat or lowered in the basket for safe fun and observation, and shares the glories of the day and the wonders of the night. Writing about the vision that night on the high seas produces, Heyerdahl comments: "Coal-black seas towered up on all sides, and a glittering myriad of tropical stars drew a faint reflection from plankton in the water. The world was simple—stars in the darkness. Whether it was 1947 B.C. or A.D. suddenly became of no significance. . . . We realized that life had been full for men before the technical age also—in fact, fuller and richer in many ways than the life of modern man" (131-32). From the rubber raft, seen in the darkness punctuated by stars, "the *Kon-Tiki* rose out of the seas to sink down again behind black masses of water that towered between her and us. In the moonlight there was a fantastic atmosphere about the raft. Stout, shining wooden logs fringed with seaweed, the square pitch-black outline of a Viking sail, a bristly bamboo hut with the yellow light of a paraffin lamp aft—the whole suggested a picture from a fairytale rather than the actual reality" (133). Time evaporates for them and yields a transcendental moment. "We could well see in our mind's eye the whole flotilla of such vessels, spread in fan formation beyond the horizon to increase the chances of finding land, when the first men made their way across this sea" (132).

There are epic touches, too, such as "when at night our glowing road guide, the sun, climbed down from the sky and disappeared beyond the sea in the west with his whole spectrum of colors, the gentle trade wind blew life into the stories of the strange mystery of Easter Island" (134). Unlike Odysseus, who is left with not even a remnant of his sailors at the end, the whole crew of the *Kon-Tiki* arrives at their destination, surviving the wreck of their raft on the perilous coral reef. Not back home and not fending off suitors, these epic heroes, however, are welcomed by the islanders in a ceremony bestowing honorary citizenship on them and rechristening them with the names of the islanders' revered forbearers. Even though the return trip is anticlimactic it rates several poetic paragraphs at the close of the book.

* * *

Also suited to those with wanderlust and thirsty for adventure, Captain James Cook's *Voyage Round the World* is a compendium of discoveries of navigational and anthropological significance. Narrated by natural historian George Forster, in an often erudite yet felicitous and surprisingly brisk style that refuses to camouflage matters obscene or horrific and, Swift-like, aims at accuracy and relies on telling detail, the translated work grips the attention of the reader. At points, however, the lengthy descriptions and investigative reporting summon patience on the part of the reader to apprehend the subject's import in its entirety. Forster drew from his own diary and assimilated material from the journals of the elder Forster and Captain Cook himself. The account, notable for its wealth of scientific, geographical, and sociological findings, is interlarded with apt quotations from classical belletrists and philosophers. The second of Cook's three main voyages, this expedition carried out with companion ships *Resolution* and *Adventure*, turned up little that was novel regarding navigation but added copious and penetrating observations of ethnological importance. The volumes are rich in information and lore concerning the islanders of the South Pacific. Like previous European explorers sanguine about prospects of finding a northwest passage, Cook and his mates failed in the attempt, finally putting to rest the chimera others had endlessly pursued. On this voyage, they established that despite persistent claims and hopes, no southern continent exists.

The fascinating and salient dimension of the work lies in its cultural perspectives regarding exotic places and peoples and their adaptation to the respective climates. Forster's book was outsold by Cook's own, more plain text, which appeared shortly after Forster's but was embellished by engravings, images, and nautical desiderata. The accounts of Cook's travels pleased Coleridge, underpinned some of the *Rime*'s navigational bearings, and colored its descriptions of polar and equatorial wonders, including perhaps the presence of the water snakes, birds, and solitary albatross featured in the haunting Romantic poem.

Forster's discursive, animated account starts in a pensive mood: "Early on Monday the 13th [of July, 1772], we set sail from Plymouth Sound, in company with the Adventure. I turned a parting look on the fertile hills of England, and gave way to the natural emotions of affection which that prospect awakened; till the beauty of the morning and the novelty of gliding through the smooth water attracted my attention, and dispersed the gloominess of former ideas" (18-19). Elsewhere he concentrates on the rigors of life and sickness and deprivation at sea, painting verbal pictures in verisimilitude, regardless of how revolting the subject. When describing the islanders, their ways, and their habitats, Forster offers contrasts and similarities from Europe to illuminate the context.

The account blends interesting details and sweeping generalizations, all marshaled by a steady narrative flow obedient to chronology and factual observation. The descriptions range from observations of the enormity of the icebergs, the dangerous fog banks mistaken for land masses, and the numbing cold of the Antarctic Circle to the consequent deterioration of the crew's health. Not left out either are observations concerning the variety of fish in the seas and of animals on the lands visited, both serving as auxiliary food sources for the men otherwise dependent on a none-too-nutritious, typically bland, and chronically rancid, even noxious diet of shipboard provisions. When they visit the islands, the salubrious climate and the abundance of meat, vegetables, and fruit restores the bodies and spirits of the men. Forster informs the reader that willing females are also available to fulfill the lust of the sex-starved sailors.

The Europeans traded necklaces of beads, iron tools and nails, and mirrors for livestock, fowl, fruits, vegetables, and, when available, bark cloth. Much bartering and exchange occurs during the island hopping. Occasionally incidents of thievery by the natives are reported. Forster also mentions, and not really under his breath, that some lower-class females were wont to surrender sex for pleasure or in payment for trinkets. Indeed, some took temporary residence on the ship during nights spent in the harbor. Forster discusses the universality of human nature and pinpoints conspicuous differences and similarities among peoples. He is not chauvinistic in presenting cultural parallels or divergence. Taboos are also noted, for example, when he encounters human cannibalism in New Zealand and dog-eating dogs on a couple of islands. By contrast, the stretches spent near the South Pole were almost entirely disagreeable. There, "we rather vegetated than lived" (293), Forster exclaims.

A stickler for detail, Forster musters endless references to the bearings and markings of the course of navigation, variations in temperatures, the condition and direction of the wind and currents, and elements attesting to the progress and underlying purpose of the voyage. He extols the accuracy of the age-old method of determining longitude by referencing the sun, moon, and stars. He concludes that cross-checking by time-keeping instruments does little to refine the process. Naturalistic minutiae abound. For instance, the description of penguins focuses on the protective insulating plumage whose density causes gunshot to ricochet. Or, as an example of the plenitude principle at work in Forster's recording of naturalistic features, take the following typical entry: "The island before us was extremely low and sandy, and formed an elliptic rocky ledge, no less than six leagues in its longest diameter, from north to south. Its latitude is 14° 28' S. and its longitude 144° 56' W. From space to space it was covered with coco-nut trees in great numbers, which had a pleasing airy look" (343). The description goes on to record details of size and variety in trees and shrubs, colorations of seawater and rocks, and other components contributing to the unique makeup of the scene. Such passages betray the writer's fondness for details of natural history. Unfortunately, at such points, the reader may experience tedium and be tempted to skim this and similar patches of excessively detailed observation and move forward to the remaining and, fortunately, characteristically lively text comprising the double-tome work.

In contrast to or as a compliment to the delineation of natural phenomena, the narrator's exposition of the mores and physical features and ways of the island people they meet is akin to what readers come across in issues of *National Geographic*. Forster's verbal pictures are as complete in fullness and detail as colored photographs. The islanders' pets, diet, jewelry, dress, customs, and manners are carefully rendered in paragraphs like silhouettes or profiles, giving close-ups to offset the views of the distant horizons that otherwise overwhelm the voyage. The brief sojourns among islanders are reliefs that add to the authenticity of the voyage felt by the reader. Each of the peoples of the islands visited is compared and contrasted with their counterparts inhabiting other islands. Their indigenous ways and cultures, facts of flora and fauna of their respective habitats, and their dress or lack thereof are likewise viewed against the perspectives of the Europeans whose civilization the travelers incarnate. This feature of comparative views is the nub of all travelogues. Often the short stops at various islands prove therapeutic to the mariners. For the duration of the stay and as long as the supplies stowed aboard upon leaving last, the men are refreshed by a diverse and salutary diet, a welcome switch from the customarily meager provisions aboard the ship. The favorable climate, landscape, and society of the tropics do wonders for their outlook and physical wellbeing. They are also introduced to the novelty of eating new foods, even dog meat. Forster celebrates the Society Islands of the Pacific, especially Tahiti. Auspicious climate, engaging, hospitable people, lush vegetation, alluring pacific setting, and atmosphere—here was a tropical paradise.

BRYSON'S EXPANDED WORLD

- A Walk in the Woods -

Besides contributing an extravagantly comic memoir of his boyhood, *The Life and Times of the Thunderbolt Kid*, a wildly imaginative chronicle of growing up in the 50s and 60s in Des Moines, Iowa, Bill Bryson has added over a dozen wonderful volumes to the library sections of travel literature and the English language. Among the travel works penned, one that fills a conspicuous gap, one close to the Cumberland Gap but highlights the Appalachian Trail (aka AT), is *A Walk in the Woods*, published in 1991. Pairing up with a latter-day Sancho Panza, a buddy from his past and now a floater, Stephen Katz, the narrator and his sidekick don backpacks, sleeping bags, and way too much camping gear to undertake on foot a 2,000-mile trek through the monumental chain of valleys and peaks meandering roughly—though said to be smooth old mountains—parallel to the Eastern seaboard. Starting in Georgia and ending up in Maine, mostly together but not always keeping apace, the two trudged along through rain, shadows, and sweat, trying to meet a quota of maybe ten miles a day. Each night they set up camp and chomp down a portion of their nearly endless supply of noodles. Finding their journey too strenuous and rationalizing that the routine has become redundant and that completing not quite half of the mileage still qualifies as a valiant attempt, they allow themselves to claim a triumph. "We hiked the Appalachian Trail" (394), the author declares on their behalf when they give up early.

The book has both humor and conservationist appeal. It makes you smile and laugh, and it causes you to think and reflect. The mix of commercialism and wilderness varies. But the message Bryson delivers is that, despite gross governmental ineptitude, humanity's inherent greed, and the American's almost ubiquitous addiction to a lazy, gadget-filled, resource-depleting lifestyle, nature, remains a valuable part of our world and our total mysterious makeup.

The book is two-halved. I find part 1, the first dozen chapters, more enthralling than Part 2, at least until chapter 19, when the hikers recommence the journey together. In Part 2, without his companion Katz, Bryson sounds more like a diarist. The first half, which consumes some 500 miles of rugged terrain, abounds in humor. The second half strikes a more sober note. In the absence of his charter companion, Bryson tackles bits of the trail solo or with another hiker or two. Instead of making a continuous and overnight trek, like other "day-hikers," he parks his car, goes off to catch a chunk of the trail, and then returns to his car and home to prepare for the next day's foray into the woods. Outstanding, literally, and by his scrupulous account of its geological history, character, and severity, is the part about Mount Washington, the coldest, windiest, though far from tallest, summit in the world. We might legitimately choose the adjective "awesome" here. The account of the era of the grand resort hotels holds our fascination. What lingers here and elsewhere in the book is a lament over the decline of nature. As he puts it, "In America, alas, beauty has become something you drive to, and nature an either/or proposition—either you ruthlessly subjugate it . . . or you deify it." He craves a state where "people and nature could coexist to their mutual benefit" (286). The loss of the songbirds and the general receding number and an array of species, plants, and animals prompts an elegiac tone. The note of regret is particularly sounded in the foreground of Part 2. Bryson's enthusiasm for the wilderness accommodates the perils lurking there but is tempered by the touristy spectaculars he encounters both on and off the trail.

When Katz and Bryson rejoin to continue their hike, the book turns decidedly comic again. Following some serious serial hikes in coal-veined Pennsylvania and the jagged White Mountains of New Hampshire, Bryson reunites with his partner for the finale "deep into the boundless woods of northern Maine for our trek through the Hundred Mile Wilderness."

The book's subtitle encapsulates the goal of "Rediscovering America on the Appalachian Trail." Like other books whose itinerary cuts a swath through the country or a portion of it, *A Walk in the Woods* gets us familiar with aspects of America that we've neglected to notice, have never known about, or need to recover an appreciation or knowledge of. In this case, however, the mode of travel is basic—covering a primitive trail by foot, inch by inch. Whether the book induces the urge to hike in the reader is perhaps moot. The armchair traveler hoofs along with the narrator, seeing and hearing what the narrator takes in and reports. Vicariously, as readers, we experience a trace of the hikers' fatigue and empathize with them at moments of exaltation counterbalanced by times of frustration and outrage. We learn about the trail and how it fits in the larger context of nature and are assisted in appreciating the scope of the planet's history back to its origins and the big changes brought about by shifting land plates, the formation and movement of glaciers, and evolutionary forces operating over an incredible time span. With the lens focused sharply on recent history and present time, we can see the potential for good and ill that human life and civilization have brought and are still imposing on the natural scene.

The book is delightfully fun. Undertaking to complete a sizable stretch of this "granddaddy of long hikes" (3), which, if he persisted, would take "about five months, and five million steps, to walk . . . from end to end" (10), Bryson lays out the reasons and rationalizations for attempting the feat. The first is, "It would get me fit after years of waddlesome sloth" (4). He is mightily aware at the outset that there are dangers galore. Everybody knows of somebody else, as he hyperbolically puts it, "who had gone off hiking the trail with high hopes and new boots and come stumbling back two days later with a bobcat attached to his head or dripping blood from an armless sleeve and whispering in a hoarse voice, '*Bear!*' before sinking into a troubled unconsciousness" (5). Other perils than ferocious animals lurking out there for convenient hosts include numerous diseases that could set in or, simply, the onslaught of unbearable—pun optional—weather. Storms, lightning bolts, excessive temperature swings—the away-from-home pals will have to contend with threats from Mother Nature. Heading out to the toolies, Bryson imagines "tents crushed beneath falling trees, or eased off precipices on ball bearings of beaded rain and sent paragliding on to distant valley floors" (6). Not to mention "hikers beyond counting whose last experience was of trembling earth and the befuddled thought 'Now what the—?'" (6) Some diseases, take Lyme disease, he announces, "If undetected, . . . can lie dormant in the human body for years before erupting in a positive fiesta of maladies" (7), which he goes on to detail with painful accuracy and a touch of humor. "Finally," he concludes the litany of likely mishaps and threats to a hiker's wellbeing or survival, "this being America, there is the constant possibility of murder" (8).

Next follows the episode at the outfitters where he buys a ton of gear and equipment under the encouragement of the veteran salesman, who both shames and overrides his customer's naïve preferences and budget, like an overbearing talk-your-head-off car dealer. To augment his survival supplies, he acquires several books to read up on the rigors, splendors, and horrors associated with hiking the trail. Some bits are gruesome reports of animals mutilating and raiding campsites and their occupants. Quite a note to start on! It isn't till late in the journey that Bryson gets a hold of a decent large-scale map. For miles, he has to sort of guess at and fill in blanks and directions to understand where they are and are not, so minute is the map, so vast the expanse, so convoluted are the twists and turns and ups and downs of the way forward. Sometimes, though surprisingly seldom, they run into other hikers. Early on, a troop of Eagle scouts trots by them to show them up by the ease with which they manage to move forward as effortlessly as the breeze as if they were creatures who had been born and raised in the wilderness. Some days later, a woman from Florida hooks up with the men and voluntarily shares their noodle feasts and sweets they've squirreled away, criticizes their hiking methods and paraphernalia, and annoys them with her non-stop chatter and odd habit of blowing out her ears. To part ways, Bryson and Katz make a point of outdistancing her one day and slip off the trail into a town to wait out the welcome separation. Upon continuing, however, and enjoying a night apart from her, they resume the trio; Mary Ellen had managed to catch up and rejoin them. A big presence in their company, "she leaned over to get something from her pack displaying an expanse of backside on which you could have projected motion pictures for, let us say, an army base" (75-76). The tension builds. Bryson reports:

"While we ate raisins and drank coffee with flecks of toilet paper in it, Mary Ellen gorged on a multicourse breakfast of oatmeal, Pop Tarts, trail mix, and a dozen small squares of chocolate, which she lined up on the log beside her. We watched like orphaned refugees while she plumped her jowls with food and enlightened us as to our shortcomings with regard to diet, equipment, and general manliness" (76). The strain ends when they successfully ditch her and treat themselves to a picnic with egg-salad sandwiches, soft drinks, and plenty of junk food to boot.

While Katz is fairly successful in staying sober during the trip, his addiction to sweets is a source of comic vignettes. Barely into the trip, determined his pack was too heavy, Katz randomly jettisons most of its contents. Somehow the noodles survived the dump. Hence, their staple for the duration was set. If I might paraphrase Coleridge's ancient mariner, it was noodles, noodles everywhere and not a lick of much else. OD-ing on noodles, they both jump at the chance to swill cream soda, snack on Snickers and Twinkies, and down fast-food burgers and fries when they can conveniently head off course and visit a village bordering the trail. The rare overnights at a cheap motel or a crowded hostel punctuate the regimen of Spartan under-the-stars or in-the-rain campouts. The marathoners endure the gamut of conditions, from the sodden and shivery to the sweaty and itchy. Many a night, they lie bundled in their bags, exhausted yet unable to sleep and refresh for the mileage looming at dawn, following the brief ritual of coffee and packing up. Though they are principally apart from others, the trip affords glimpses of the parade of humanity. When they stop at an available shelter for a modicum of R & R, an account of those present is rendered. The portraits Bryson sketches and his script of the little dramas enacted, including oddments of dialogue and actions, provide comic interludes counterpointing their struggles and chuckles as they persevere, a pair of determined but novice hikers.

The ever-present trees, where logging or disease hasn't obliterated them, or they've grown back, stand as protagonists of the journey. The terrain and weather serve not so much as antagonists as formidable agents respected and admired for their natural ways. The men have set themselves a quest; they are answering a call to nature, summoned to the wilderness to test their mettle and meet the mental and physical challenge of a lifetime. Theirs is hardly the proverbial walk in the park.

It is an arduous walk in venerable woods, a walk a sedentary reader can enjoy reading about and perhaps ponder whether to set out on such an adventure for real. As with Bunyan in *Pilgrim's Progress,* Twain in *A Tramp Abroad,* Theroux in *A Kingdom by the Sea,* and many other travelogues, Bryson's journey involves a marathon of hoofing it. Quite rightly, as he notes, "Distance changes utterly when you take the world on foot" (100). The bittersweet novelty of the book and the chosen mode of travel lies in the fact that too seldom do modern Americans walk, owing in part to the difficulty of walking in a land largely remade and dedicated to vehicular traffic.

Touring America in a vehicle as do Heat-Moon in *Blue Highways* and Steinbeck in *Travels with Charley* before him but in a small car rather than a pickup or camper, Bryson, as he chronicles in an earlier book, also sets out to find the heart and feel the pulse of the country. In crossing America, all three travelers avoid freeways and take to the side roads wherever possible. In *The Lost Continent: Travels in Small-Town America,* published in 1989, Bryson is in search of Amalgam, his term for the quintessential small town he had known as a boy and come to romanticize as an adult. His idealization of small-town America was fixated after a sojourn of nearly twenty years living in England. Such a town, Amalgam, would comprise all or many components identified with life in the ideal town. In his quest, he runs across many disappointments. However, he does find candidates with a sampling of the desired down-to-earth traits: a thriving main street with a mom-and-pop grocery store, a genuine dime store, a drug store with a soda fountain, a couple of cafes, an old-fashioned movie theatre, and other locally owned and uniquely named businesses. It wouldn't smack of franchises, corporate sameness, and strip malls. Rather, it would be a community of people who aren't in a rush and are glad to take time to get acquainted and offer help, folks connected and their regular activities of school, work, church, local politics, and gossip. Ironically, Bryson discovers that the closer he gets back to where he started, in Des Moines, Iowa, the more he feels at home and immersed in the welcome experience he remembers.

In Bryson's travelogue, teeming with humor, much of it of the self-deprecatory variety, he scores with comparisons. Not able to be served a meal at the only open restaurant in Sundance, Wyoming, because the

Shriners have monopolized the establishment by reservation, he has two options besides starving. The waitress informs him that there is a Tastee-Freez way out of town or a gas station up the street where he can purchase potato chips, candy bars, and a soft drink. Deprived of a decent supper of standard restaurant fare, he spends that Saturday night in a rundown motel, filling up on treats. As he puts it, "I lay there [watching some nonsense on TV] and pushed candy bars into my face, like logs into a sawmill" (285).

Generalizing at the outset about his and others' origins and aspirations, he writes: "I come from Des Moines. Somebody had to. When you come from Des Moines you either accept the fact without question and settle down with a local girl named Bobbi and get a job at the Firestone factory and live there forever and ever, or you spend your adolescence moaning at length about what a dump it is and how you can't wait to get out, and then you settle down with a local girl named Bobbi and get a job at the Firestone factory and live there forever and ever" (3). In Garrison Keiller's Lake Wobegon, "all the women are strong, all the men are good-looking, and all the children are above average." According to Bryson, the trademark or birthmark of his hometown is that everybody there, except Mr. Piper, an unlucky man who drank too much and was always getting a car out of the body shop and who denigrated foreigners and Democrats, "is strangely serene" (3).

The Lost Continent and Bryson's other travel books will appeal to the reader of *A Walk in the Woods*. For Bryson packs each full of information and amusing sidelights, all narrated in an easily negotiated, animated style, with plenty of figurative surprises, apt allusions, and fitting slang to keep the reader engaged and moving along.

DANA "BEFORE THE MAST"

A quick read and simultaneously a vicarious workout, Richard Dana's *Two Years Before the Mast*, published in 1840, chronicles a route familiar and dangerous for many clipper ships, brigs, and other craft. Completing the Panama Canal in 1914, connecting the Caribbean Sea with the Pacific Ocean, would constitute a sea change of great magnitude. It would archive the challenging intercontinental voyage that was the passage of necessity over the centuries. For it would divert traffic away from the ice-jams and storms of the Cape and save precious time moving cargo between the Atlantic and the Pacific. But that vastly shorter and safer route was still way in the offing when Dana lived, sailed, and wrote his historical account.

The author left college and embarked on a voyage to save his failing eyesight. He hoped by a furlough at sea to relieve his sore eyes, see the world, and pursue his education in a different vein before returning to Boston to complete his degree, study law, and become a lawyer. It was not a pleasure cruise. Dana stuck it out for two years.

During his stint at sea, he mastered the chores, chants, and nomenclature currently aboard big sailing vessels. As is evident in the text, a glorified version of the diary and memories he kept, he persevered and even reveled in the work of maintaining the ship's sails and course of navigation and the arduous toil demanded of seamen. He did wince, understandably, at the punishment a high-handed captain inflicted on two obstinate, well-intentioned mates who maintained their rights in the face of bad calls by the captain. The friendships Dana made, off-shore duties, and short-lived pleasures during rare free time are intriguingly described.

Dana, a straight arrow, never shrinks from doing what is asked or expected of him on or off the ship. On board, when not sailing, crew-members carried out periodic chores such as tarring the spars and masts, "picking oakum," coiling the rigging, scrubbing and painting the decks, and repairing the sails and yards—keeping all shipshape. Only when he is seriously sick and extremely weak from an abscessed tooth, and can't hold down any food, is Dana excused from responsibilities for a week till he heals and recovers his strength. Then he feels guilty for having not done his share of the work. In rough weather in the South Pole regions, Dana and his crew mates do their best in the icy cold with hands numb and hardly able to function and clothes frozen from sweat and sleet. During horrendous weather, they try to catch short rests below deck in their wet togs for brief intervals between shifts or "watches." Dana is a trooper who performs yeoman's service when assigned shore duty to gather, carry, cure, and load hundreds of hides. The same is true of the wood-gathering expeditions he and a fellow crew member were called on to undertake. They were like diversions. "These wooding excursions," he reports, "had always a mixture of something rather pleasant in them. Roaming about the woods with hatchet in hand, like a backwoodsman, followed by a troop of dogs; starting up of birds, snakes, hares and foxes, and examining the various kinds of trees, flowers, and birds' nests, was at least, a change from the monotonous drag and pull on shipboard" (154).

Episodes of pleasure when ashore and off duty consisted of horse-back riding, indulging in a few drinks, and enjoying camaraderie with the other workers in the "ovens" and hide camps, most of whom had come from distant lands and spoke foreign languages. In Santa Barbara, then a coastal village, two ceremonial interludes occur. On Easter, Dana and several friends witness a funeral procession for a young girl and are intrigued by its being more jubilant than solemn. Carrying on the tradition, the family and friends spent the previous evening reveling and dancing. On the way to the church, the casket was borne by girls dressed in white and in high spirits, two men, repeatedly shooting their muskets, escorted the entourage. Again, in Santa Barbara, a few weeks after the Christmas holidays, Dana is among those who go ashore to participate in an elaborate Catholic wedding for their ship's agent and the daughter of a leading family of old California. The nuptial festivities include joyous dancing and the breaking of cologne-filled eggs on the heads of unsuspecting eligible bachelors by flirtatious eager-to-be-courted young women. Dana also visits an old mission in San Diego and other historical sites in various coastal towns destined to become world ports. In his spare time, Dana teaches himself Spanish and consequently learns more about the Californians' manners, customs, and culture, including their architecture, furnishings, beliefs, and pastimes.

Throughout, the discipline and confinement of seafaring underpin Dana's emerging definition of liberty. One comes to know more exactly and appreciate more fully a thing or state of being by the exaggeration or loss of its opposite. Such was the narrator's happiness at a well-earned and novel moment of freedom from the ongoing bondage of seafaring.

> I shall never forget the delightful sensation of being in the open air [on land], with the birds singing around me, and escaped from the confinement, labor, and strict rule of a vessel—of being once more in my life, though only for a day, my own master. A sailor's liberty is but for a day; yet while it lasts it is perfect. He is under no one's eye, and can do whatever, and go wherever, he pleases. This day, for the first time, I may truly say, in my whole life, I felt the meaning of a term which I had often heard—the sweets of liberty. (114-15)

The effect of freedom from incessant toil was like a taste of a rare wine by a discerning pauper. Dana could return to drudgery with a fresh perspective: "It was wonderful how the prospect brightened, and how short and tolerable the voyage appeared, when viewed in this new light. Things looked differently from what they did when we talked them over in the little dark forecastle, the night after the flogging at San Pedro" (115).

Though not exactly in a Robinson Crusoe situation, Dana is equally resourceful and self-reliant. Often alone in thought, he is, however, not a solitary figure but a gregarious young man who ungrudgingly follows through on assigned tasks and genuinely enjoys the company of his fellow sailors and persons with whom he becomes acquainted ashore.

Memorable, too, are the welcomed moments when the crew is allowed to tend to personal matters. Under the command of the harsh

Captain Thompson, aboard the Pilgrim, Sunday was not regularly a day of leisure. Yet, occasionally, as a respite from the long hours of toil, a brief period would be set aside for communal, "grand washing" and mending of clothes and bedding and bathing. But, of course, only after the swabbing and scouring of the decks had been done. Rainwater made a treat out of laundering and bathing. How simple the chore, how wonderful the effect! Dana notes,

> "A little fresh water, which we had saved from our allowance, was put in buckets, and with soap and towels, we had what sailors call a fresh-water wash. . . . After this, came shaving, and combing, and brushing; and when, having spent the first part of the day in this way, we sat down on the forecastle, in the afternoon, with clean duck trousers, and shirts on, washed, shaved, and combed, and looking a dozen shades lighter for it, reading, sewing, and talking at our ease, with a clear sky and warm sun over our heads, a steady breeze over the larboard quarter, studding-sails out alow and aloft, and all the flying kites aboard;—we felt that we had got back into the pleasantest part of a sailor's life" (327-28).

Such interludes of fellowship and solitude provided a tonic to keep going, continue sailing, and endure the voyage's hardships and rigor.

The contrasts between the world of the sailors and life off the boat and between what life was remembered back East and what it is like on the California coast make for interesting observations. Another source of interest arises from the contrast between the initially bewildering orders shouted out to the new mariner and the later ease with which the narrator, once trained, delineates all the ship's stations, names all the sails, and invokes the appropriate navigational terms and devices. The nautical knowledge and experience he gains on the working voyage contribute to the authenticity of the travelogue. In recounting the voyage, he is well-equipped to accurately describe and define their progress sailing both stern and friendly winds and waves. The arrivals at various harbors and the maneuvering in and coping with the intricacies of anchoring follow the manual and transition to topics of wrap-up duties aboard and, if granted leave, activities unfolding ashore.

Dana is adept at delineating different processes associated with his time spent at sea and on shore. We get a clear and instructive picture of the work involved in collecting, cleaning, curing, hauling, and loading the hides to be brought back East, replacing cargo from the voyage out. As a commercial ship, they traded such articles as coffee and tea, spices, dishes and utensils, hardware and tools, clothing and shoes, fabrics, jewelry, furniture, and—literally—"everything that can be imagined, from Chinese fireworks to English cart-wheels" (78). Time and labor were spent row-boating goods and customers from shore to ship and back to shore again. Dana picks up on the personality of old California, the days before the Gold Rush, and the movement westward of Americans of predominantly European extraction. Back then, it was but "a half-civilized coast, at the ends of the earth" (92), a long way from Boston and home.

The daily diet of the common seamen consisted of dried beef or salt pork, hard biscuits, and tea. No wonder when on shore, they bartered for potatoes and other vegetables, which foods supplied needed nutrition and helped ward off scurvy. The ship's cook occasionally regales the crew with a concoction of plum pudding or rice with molasses. The standard menu was grim and monotonous.

Dana traces—and, more interestingly, dramatizes—the hierarchy on the ship. From the captain, orders descend to the chief mate, second mate, steward, cook, and crew, charged with manning and repairing the sails, lines, mast, and rigging. The crew's Spartan quarters occupied crannies "before the mast" (or in front of and below, to translate the nautical jargon). Their labor was measured out in two- and four-hour watches round the clock.

Dana pinpoints the mixed emotions felt when, rare on the high seas but happily more frequent along the coast, encountering another ship at sea, pirate or friend, foreign or domestic. On the troubling side, he experienced silent lament when death occurred at sea, caused by a mate succumbing to disease, being swept off the deck in a violent gale, or, by a missed step or reach, plummeting from an upper sail. The loss when the livestock washed overboard was twofold: the foregone fresh meat and the forsaken society the animals had provided. Becoming almost pets, penned in lifeboats and a makeshift sty and a coop, and daily a familiar visible, audible, and quite smelly presence, they were sincerely missed.

When the animals were present, the ship could have passed for a version of Noah's Ark or even a floating peaceable kingdom. Regrettably, when the chickens, bullocks, sheep, and pigs vanished in the deep, it left only fish to supplement the salty meat rations.

Dana makes the reader feel a part of the action as if numbered among the crew members. Capturing the thrill of rapid sailing, he writes: "The starboard watch hauled aft the sheet, and the ship tore through the water like a mad horse, quivering and shaking at every joint, and dashing from its head the foam, which flew off at every blow, yards and yards to leeward. A half hour of such sailing served our turn, when the clews of the sail were hauled up, the sail furled, and the ship, eased of her press, went more quietly on her way" (200). It doesn't matter if a few of the terms have to be guessed at. We are taken in by the spirit and acceleration of the wind's force on the brig forging ahead in the foam-crested ocean waves. It could as well be Homer or Coleridge as Dana at the helm.

The account unfolds chronologically. It takes five months and fifty pages to reach the California coast. Nearly a year is consumed going in and out of harbors, trading and gathering cargo and supplies for the return voyage. The second year away, Dana's home ship having returned to San Pedro after five months' separation from its onboard duties to assist in the hide-loading endeavor, takes up half the book's length. The final segment of the journey, which reverses the route out, offers distinctive challenges and experiences—all narrated in lively prose, punctuated with snatches of dialogue and accompanying descriptions. The remaining half-year, during which Dana is engaged in preparations for and completing the homeward journey, runs out the final hundred pages or last third of the book.

When it appears that his sojourn at sea may extend beyond the two years he had allotted and possibly result in his remaining a deckhand for life, Dana manages to gain permission to transfer to the *Alert*, a vessel bound for Boston much sooner. The bargain involves finishing his job on the southern California coast, getting and loading the cargo of hides that the *Pilgrim* was slated to take back to Boston later. When suddenly orders are reversed, he has to get a sailor assigned to another ship to agree to switch places with him, which he succeeds in doing. Dana's return voyage on the *Alert* barely escapes shipwreck due to the perilous winter weather off the Cape. The several attempts to backtrack and make it through the straits are vividly depicted. Confronting the ice masses poses difficulties that slow down the progress and threaten the safety of the ship and crew. The descriptions of the icebergs, stormy blasts, and the cold mountainous waves overwhelming the ship are spectacular and foreboding.

The travelogue ends where it began, in Boston Harbor. The sentiments of homecoming differ markedly from those experienced in setting out, largely because of the narrator's having secured his sought-after remedy to his eye ailment but also owing to his coming of age. Not that Dana claims to have achieved maturity. But the fulfillment of the mission at sea bolstered his intentions to return and complete his college studies—as well, of course, to write and publish the account of his journey. The voyage shaped his outlook and fostered his general sympathy for seamen and humanity. The plight of the men he had shared time with was also his plight for the duration of the voyage. Their hardships were his hardships. However, unlike his erstwhile companions, Dana had the good fortune to move on beyond the waves.

The narrator's coming of age is afforded not just by a fact of chronology or by the act of once or twice crossing the Equator (or coming and going four times) or rounding Cape Horn. The experiences at sea shared with mates aboard the ship are laden with implications, chief among them his having contributed to their happening and the realization that he bears some of the responsibility for the crew's survival and the safe transportation of the goods aboard. Learning to deal with nature's assaults—snow, hail, sleet, scorching heat or intense cold and the roughness of the seas and fickleness and force of the wind—constitutes a vital arena of accomplishment and growth. The strict discipline imposed by the captain, combined with the fatigue endured during the watches and required maintenance of the vessel as well as any assigned shore duties, posed attendant challenges. His sojourn at sea called for physical stamina, intelligence, and, at times, the capacity to escape by reading, reflecting, or hobnobbing with others in the same boat. It was, in effect, a kind of intense internship.

En route, Dana summarizes the requirements and special character, the macho bravado, manifested by sailors. He writes:

> An overstrained sense of manliness is the characteristic of seafaring men, or, rather, of life on board ship. This often gives an appearance of want of feeling, and even of cruelty. From this, if a man comes within an ace of breaking his neck and escapes, it is made a joke of; and no notice must be taken of a bruise or a cut; and any expression of pity, or any show of attention, would look sisterly, and unbecoming a man who has to face the rough and tumble of such a life. From this, too, the sick are neglected at sea, and whatever sailors may be ashore, a sick man finds little sympathy or attention, forward or aft. A man, too, can have nothing peculiar or sacred on board ship; for all the nicer feelings they take pride in disregarding, both in themselves and others. A thin-skinned man could not live an hour on shipboard. One would be torn raw unless he had the hide of an ox. (249)

One of Dana's numerous close-up portraits—grist for any tale of travel—is that of his watch-mate for nine months, Tom Harris. "The most remarkable man I have ever seen," he declares, commenting on Tom's perfect memory. "He carried in his head not only a log-book of the whole voyage, in which everything was complete and accurate . . . but also an accurate registry of all the cargo" (191). Dana praises the man's uncanny ability to precisely calculate "the hoist of every mast, and spread of every sail" (192). His entire life history, every place he had been, all the persons whom he had met, "the name of every sailor that had ever been his shipmate, and also, of every vessel, captain, and officer, and the principal dates of each voyage" (193)—Tom could instantly retrieve. In addition, he had an astounding sense of logic to match his absolute recall of events and conversations. Dana marvels, "He knew every lunar star in both hemispheres, and was a perfect master of his quadrant and sextant. Such was the man, who, at forty, was still a dog before the mast, at twelve dollars a month" (194). We also learn of Tom's past life of indulgence—"Every sin that a sailor knows he had gone to the bottom of" (195). However, when Dana met Tom, who had a few years earlier become sober, with a great resolve never to drink or carry on as in the past, he benefited from having a valuable model and mentor to follow and a friend indeed.

Among adventures on land, Dana tells of their flinging hides over a cliff one time and watching them soar out into the air and dive down, but then he has to rappel the precipice like a cragsman to retrieve a bunch of them that got caught halfway down in a crevice. Generally, they employed mules or carts to transport the hides, once stretched and dried in the sun. This time, though, for a lark and what appeared to be a shortcut, had tried another, more novel means.

He reports that the hardest part of the work comes in toting the heavy hides on their heads and sloshing out to pitch them into the boat. Dana is ever one to complete the mission, whatever the risk and difficulty. His "two years before the mast" is some working holiday! Though he laments the abuses inflicted by tyrannical captains and commiserates with the seamen whose workload and conditions are hardly bearable, he remains exuberant and celebrates the elemental joy of mastering the craft of sailing with his teammates. As readers and wannabe sailors, we identify with and learn much from Dana's multifaceted excursion at sea.

TRAVELING *BLUE HIGHWAYS*

A trip is defined by *how* you go, your travel mode, and *where* you go. In *Blue Highways,* published in 1982, William Least Heat-Moon heads for the back roads in his 1975 Ford van, dubbed "Ghost Dancing" after an Indian ceremony undertaken to bring back a way of life that was vanishing. The book traces a three-month, 13,000-mile route around, not just across, America, going out of his way to patronize small-town cafés and bars or to stop for a spell at your old-time roadhouse and chat with locals to get to know the idiosyncrasies of American life. For starters, take this tidbit as a representative excerpt: "Not so much to eat as to occupy myself, I went into a no-name, three-calendar, ten-stool café with walls of linoleum. Idling, I asked the cook who lifted hot lids with her apron ends, 'What's the name of your diner?'" (327). And thereby, a particular conversation gets underway.

The author's penchant for comparisons is a constant source of interest and delight for the reader of *Blue Highways.* Various intriguing similes and metaphors capture the nuances of the landscapes and personalities he encounters. Like so many other travelers who liken their trip to one thing or another, at one point, he compares his trip to "the bear going over the mountain to see what he could see" (397). The book is replete with comparisons and word pictures that treat our imaginations and zero in on the identity of things witnessed along the way. A few examples, all registering the sound of the human voice, whet the thirst for figurative language: "he said in a voice like a truck in low gear" (78); "her voice was deep and soft like water moving in a cavern" (77); "a man with a voice hollow like the drip of water in an empty pan complained" (362); "he ducked inside as if my words were stones" (374). An expression is preserved in a single verbal swish of the painter's brush: "I asked a man, whose brow opened and closed like a concertina as he talked, what was going on" (194). A hitchhiker he picks up has skin that "shone like wet delta mud" and a smile that "glittered like a handful of new dimes" (109). A woman in Georgia who was "an authority" on everything is accorded alliterative stops. "Her face, pallid like a partly boiled potato, looked as if carved out with a paring knife" (91-92). In the ensuing episode, the author identifies her with the epithet "The potato had just said" (92). Every mile of the trip, every page recounting the journey, is loaded with fetching details and curious observations, all clothed with words appropriate and unique to the occasion.

We read, "In the approaching car beams, raindrops spattering the road became little beacons" (6); "mostly we poured down ice tea and hung in our chairs like damp rags" (307); "clean as a Norwegian kitchen" (278); "the road climbed so far above the river valley that barns looked like Monopoly hotels" (230). Some descriptions are layered in comparisons like fine agates, drawn from the depths of knowledge or thrown out as if come upon most naturally. They seem spontaneous, not studied. Here is one: "He just looked at me, his brown eyes shining like pocket-worn chestnuts, his head a creased, leathery bag that might have been dug from a Danish peat bog" (290). Heat-Moon's comparisons both draw from and add to the reader's realm of experience. In his company, the traveler moves over familiar territory and goes beyond, buoyed forward by the power of images. The contours of faces and towns are caught by repeated strokes of an imaginative brush dipping a palette held close.

Consider how a single town is remembered by a homely image wrested from childhood play that ekes fun and fantasy out of broken bits. "Kewaunee, sitting on the eastern base of the peninsula that separated the inlet called Green Bay from the open lake, had a business district just a few feet above the water, with homes a hundred feet higher on sheer cliffs that dropped to the shore. It was as if someone had broken a mixing bowl in half, built a toy town in the bottom, and put little houses on the rim" (288-9). Elsewhere, "Like bony fingers, three mesas reached down from larger Black Mesa into the middle of Hopi land" (175). At another spot, the road, after going every which way, straightened out, "like a chalkline" (189). Sketching the whim of a meandering stream,

Heat-Moon observed, "But, worse than flooding, the Rio Grande, like a wandering burro, would change course without warning" (153).

Understandably, the subject of blue highways vs. interstates surfaces quite a lot. The following passages come early on and set our expectations for the kinds of events and meetings to be narrated:

> The tumult of St. Louis behind, the Illinois superwide quiet but for the rain, I turned south onto state 4, a shortcut to I-64. After that, the 42,500 miles of straight and wide could lead to hell for all I cared: I was going to stay on the three million miles of bent and narrow rural American two-lane, the roads to Podunk and Toonerville. Into the sticks, the boondocks, the burgs, backwaters, jerkwaters, the wide-spots-in-the-road, the don't-blink-or-you'll-miss-it towns. Into those places where you say, 'My God! What if you lived here!' The Middle of Nowhere. . . . (6)
>
> U.S. 60, running from Norfolk, Virginia, to Los Angeles, used to be a major east-west route. But Interstate 64 now has taken up the heavy traffic and left 60 to farm pickups and kids on horses. For the blue highway traveler, freeing roads like this one is the purpose of the interstates. Comprising only one percent of American highways, the interstate system has opened a lot of roadway to the dawdler. (14)

To the extent that this book, like many travel books, is a gazetteer, it offers the added enjoyment of discovering geographical oddities and nomenclature. Heat-Moon's flair for caricature in defining the essence of particular towns and regions is a source of amusement and interest. We linger spellbound over pictures he paints of Frankfort, Kentucky; Nameless, Tennessee; Dime Box, Texas; Cedar Breaks, Utah; Austin, Nevada; Portland, Oregon; Kennebunkport, Maine; Appalachia; and towns rimming the Ohio River. Describing the contour-free northern prairies and fertile plains, he writes:

> Onward across the appallingly featureless yonder of North Dakota where towns, like the poor verse of Burma Shave signs, came and went quickly; on across fields where farmers planted wheat, rye, barley, and flax, their tractors sowing close to fences marking off

> missile silos that held Minutemen waiting in the dark underground like seeds of another sort. As daylight went, the men, racing rain and the short growing season, switched on headlights to keep the International Harvesters moving over cropland that miracles of land-grant colleges (cross-pollinated hybrids resistant to everything but growth and petrochemicals) had changed forever. The farmer's enemy wasn't a radar blip—it was the wild oat. (274)

En route, we note and revel in how much mileage the author gets out of his use of figurative language and specific details.

Names are often like little stories, Western Union messages that speak volumes and highlight momentous or just everyday incidents. Sometimes Heat-Moon spills out a catalog of choice names; other times, one name sits alone, self-conscious about its built-in history, absurdity, or ability to serve as a lens for seeing things below the surface, even implications unintended by the christeners. While traveling these blue highways, the reader cannot resist picking up a pencil to make a mark when coming across an intriguing name so that it can be retrieved to enjoy in review or share with other readers.

Heat-Moon's depiction of people as individuals, even 'characters,' derives partly from his finely tuned ear for apt dialogue. Among unforgettable utterances are those of the man who declares, "Junk's a modrun invention," and who mentions his upcoming appointment with "a tooth dentist" (47-8). Many other snatches of dialogue contain humor or have just the right idiomatic ring to them. Linguistically, his work documents a rich diversity of dialects and regionalisms still found in the USA, though steadily losing currency with the general leveling brought about by the media and society's increasing mobility.

Another technique of characterization found in the work is the rendering of a distinctive gesture or pose, as, for example, in the following sentence: "On one slanting porch, a woman worked at her wringer washer and on another a man sat at the ready with a flyswatter" (70). The power of a single item, be it an article of clothing or some other possession, to concretize a person's personality or way of life is instantly evident, for example, in the author's remark about a guy "whose cap told me what fertilizer he used" 97). Such attention to the telling detail is in the tradition of Chaucer's "General Prologue," a gallery where we are presented with the portraits of some nine-and-twenty pilgrims who will take their turn telling the stories that make up *The Canterbury Tales*. It is also a touch of Dickens.

As a former professor, the writer betrays his continuing love affair with college campuses by stopping at them, usually for breakfast and chatting in the cafeteria. He connects with all sorts—retirees, barbers, farmers, ranchers, cowboys, fishermen, auto mechanics, waitresses, bartenders, teachers, librarians, pilots, priests, miners, teamsters, gas station attendants, motel proprietors, police officers—people from all walks of life, diverse in their stated political and religious beliefs, their philosophies of life, and their take on what they or others are doing. Quite a mural of American life!

As one would expect, the book is also a running commentary on road and weather conditions, for such considerations are—sometimes have to be—uppermost for drivers of private vehicles or public conveyances, particularly if on a marathon trip. Similarly, assorted maps and road signs are observed. Occasionally an imaginary newspaper headline is invoked.

All trips are undertaken for a purpose. The chief and contributory factors prompting the author to undertake the journey are disclosed, usually directly and at the outset. The author is interested in sharing what has been learned. The tale of travel is the medium for communicating the purposes and value underlying the journey.

Unlike stories with plots where the sequence is important, some books can be read and appreciated for their parts. One can skim in places, concentrate in others, and not be seriously cheated as one definitely would be, say, in skipping around in a novel or mystery. Travel books lend themselves to window shopping. The desultory reader, the one who slackens or quickens the pace according to the interest of the scenery, the effectiveness of the author's style, or the magnetism of particular vignettes, can have a field day in books like *Blue Highways*. They typically make a good read, wherever one's eyes alight, regardless of the placement of the chapter or the connection of events. Suppose one does not care to plod away at all four-hundred plus pages and does not want to limit the sample arbitrarily or faithfully to the first hundred pages or is not keen on randomly shifting from one spot to another, guided by the relative lure of the table of contents. In that case, one is at liberty to spend the quota—since it's a pig in the poke anyway—concentrating on the selected sections. The same advice holds for later readings when one returns to linger in favorite places. In *Blue Highways*, I find myself going back to the following high points: all of Part One, "Eastward;" the first several chapters of Part Four, "South by Southwest;" most of Part Five, "West by Southwest;" and Parts Nine and Ten, "East by Northwest" and "Westward" respectively. Of course, no penalty for reading the book in its entirety or skimming the stuff between the segments proffered for closer attention. I have found that each trip builds its own momentum and tends to engross us as an entity rather than as separable items of focus.

If a trip master wins our allegiance once, we will likely sign on again, for a reread or another title by the same taleteller. Well worth the taking is the journey Heat-Moon narrates in a later book entitled *River-Horse*. It is an account of a voyage across America, linking the Hudson River, the Erie Canal, the Great Lakes, the Ohio, Mississippi, Missouri, and Columbia Rivers. At the end of his navigation, he pours a bottle of Eastern water into the Western waters, uniting the Atlantic and Pacific Oceans. Sound like a liquid successor to the Golden Spike? His most recent travel book bears the curiosity-prompting title of *Roads to Quoz: An American Mosey*."

ON THE RAILS WITH PAUL THEROUX

Paul Theroux begins his travelogue of a four-month journey to and through Asia and back, *The Great Railway Bazaar* (1975), with the beckoning call of the train. As he leaves London for passage to Paris and then eastbound for the Orient, he ponders its whistle wistfully, the sound of its thudding and whirring along the rails, steel sliding on steel. The account of the intercontinental journey taken on various connecting trains, each packed with passengers, records the interstices of the space spent on tracks in the company of fellow travelers. "I sought trains; I found passengers" (2), he announces after cataloging the series of trains—all with exotic names of the places they connected—that would make up the epic trip, his "Great Railway Bazaar," as he entitled it.

The first of the narrator's associations revolves around a man named Duffill, who was on his way to Istanbul and with whom Theroux would be sharing a compartment. Others he notices among the throng aboard are "hikers, returning Continentals with Harrods shopping bags, salesmen, French girls with sour friends, and gray-haired English couples who appeared to be embarking, armloads of novels, on expensive literary adulteries" (2). Departing from London, the view out the window changes to open countryside, interrupted only by the darkness of an occasional tunnel and, at the stations they whiz by, the faces of schoolboys and impatient drivers in cars stopped at the crossings. The sights observed in England are, of course, familiar and characteristically idiosyncratic: "Past the hopfields that gave Kent a Mediterranean tangle in September; past a Gypsy camp, fourteen battered caravans, each one with its own indestructible pile of rubbish just outside the front door; past a farm and, forty feet away, the perimeter of a housing estate with lots of interesting clothes on the line: plus fours, long johns, napping black brassieres, the pennants of bonnets and socks, all forming an elaborate message, like signal flags on the distressed convoy of those houses" (3).

True to the sensation of a traveler, actual or vicarious, upon leaving the familiar and the various that home offers and heading out to the new and the different, the consideration arising is invariably one of comparison. The novelties encountered are accommodated by their departure from and welcomed addition to the old. The transition occurring at the outset of the journey becomes duplicated and deepened the farther the trip proceeds from the point of origin, and the more it unfolds scenes and experiences of foreign places. For Theroux, chief among the fresh and the foreign are his fellow passengers, whose salient features he silhouettes as if he were Chaucer ticking off the separate traits of the nine-and-twenty horseback pilgrims accompanying him to Canterbury. Riding the *Direct-Orient Express* leaving Paris, Theroux, ready with notepad and pencil, intent upon limning the passing landscapes and sketching his gallery of portraits, lists his adjacent fellow passengers. Among them is a man "in his indignant late fifties" (12), "wearing a turtleneck, a seaman's cap, and a monocle" (10), who offers him a drink and engages him in conversation. Next on the list is a woman who reluctantly speaks a little English before smugly returning to her superior French. Also accompanying is "a Belgian girl of extraordinary size" (10) and other assorted figures, each with a different destination but joined together by the rails till they alight at their ticketed arrival stations. Molesworth, the man with a monocle, quick to share his drinks and opinions with Theroux, confesses that, based on his previous travels in India, he found "that there were many Indians who were so well bred you could treat them as absolute equals" (12).

The novelist in Theroux is everywhere evident and contributes to the reader's enjoyment as the tale of travel unwinds. In the Alps, he observed, "in the sheerest places wide-roofed chalets were planted, as close to the ground as mushrooms and clustered in the same way at various distances from gravity-defining churches. . . . At ground level the train passed fruit farms and clean villages and Swiss cycling in kerchiefs, calendar scenes that you admire for a moment before feeling an urge to move on to a new month" (15). On each leg of the trip, Theroux comments on the services available—or, more frequently, lacking—on the train he happens to be riding. He gets used to the menus and their monotony and in their absence or for a change in diet, improvises by hastily picking up provisions at junction stops. There is the American couple who, unaware that their train is not equipped with a dining car, misinterpret a brief random interruption at their compartment, imagining with the help of their appetites that it had been a call to breakfast, and are nonplussed to learn they wouldn't be served any breakfast. Theroux comments, under his breath, "Hunger's ear is not finely tuned" (15). As we know all too clearly from experience, many a traveler gets upset over changes to the routine and the expected and refuses to roll with the punches, unable to do as the Romans do.

Passing through a tunnel, a sensation compounding the claustrophobic quarters and heightening the bodily senses to ambient scents, the narrator observes fancifully: "We might be dropping down a well, a great sink-hole in the Alps that would land us in the clockwork interior of Switzerland, glacial cogs and ratchets and frostbitten cuckoos" (16). The text is laced with humor. When he questions his cabin partner as to what his plans are for his two-month stay in Turkey, Duffill shoots back a question as an answer, "'Me?'" Theroux interjects risibly for the reader, "As if the compartment was crammed with old men bound for Turkey, each waiting to state a reason" (17). Later on, when Duffill fails to get back on the train in time at a stopping point, Theroux, in a witty turn of functional shift, makes a verb of his name; jokingly with another passenger with whom he becomes chummy, he refers to similar instances of confusion as being "duffilled" (21).

The windows that Theroux stares out as the trains speed along become his camera lens or canvas. His palette of paints, the words chosen to create the brilliant cavalcade of images, conveys the ever-changing outdoor panorama of the journey to the Orient. He shares the experience with the reader by way of words and phrases and comparisons that capture the variegated scenery of the passing farms, the bicyclists with loaded bales of hay balanced precariously, the weary men off in the fields plowing with oxen, the women in kerchiefs toiling nearby or alone in their gardens, the acres and acres of vegetation, wild or domestic, and the level or undulating terrain of desert or forest. The stretch of the landscape he sees in Turkey is "but a dreary monotony of unambitious hills" (32). The foothills in Iran "were brown and scorched, like overbaked pie crust" (53). The town of Simla, in India, "fits the ridge like a saddle made entirely of rusty roofs," but, surreal like, its "fringes seemed to be sliding into the valley" (109). As the trains approach cities, the farms morph into suburbs, which give way to high-rise buildings, mosques, bridges, and myriads, even millions of people. In Istanbul, the traveler walks the city, ancient and modern. There and elsewhere, Theroux meets up with writers and academicians and is scheduled for a guest lecture on some aspect of literature.

Much of the force and memory of the book reside in similes and comparisons, both lengthy and terse. On one train are three Australians "sharing a loaf of bread, hunched over it like monkeys, two boys and a pop-eyed girl" (56). In Malaysia, "The stations raced by: Bidor, Trolak, Tapah, and Klang—names like science fiction planets" (226). Comparative summations of the traveler are as instructive as they are alluring. One such nugget is the following: "As Calcutta smells of death and Bombay of money, Bangkok smells of sex" (213). Another regards an uninviting old hotel he stays at in Ipoh, which Theroux is sure "has a skeleton in every closet and a register thick with the pseudonyms of adulterers" (225). Or try to forget the off-putting sight and stench of people and unpenned animals squatting to defecate on the tracks or by a bush; "One curious group—a man, a boy, a pig—were in a row, each shitting in his own way" (137).

Breakfasts and dinners, from humble to grand, are detailed in crisp prose. Improvised meals, particularly on the trains with limited facilities, are described, however slim or unappetizing. Eating, drinking and smoking, reading or talking, and sleeping, often fitfully due to the clatter of rain or the noise of the train or the disturbance of passengers shouting or shuffling about, all share the allotted space of the book. If it is a splendid meal of local distinction, the menu is presented in toto: "There were eight or nine dishes: *pakora*, vegetables fried in batter; *poha*, a rice mixture with peas, coriander, and turmeric; *khira*, a creamy pudding of rice, milk, and sugar; a kind of fruit salad, with cucumber and lemon added to it, called *chaat*; *murak*, a Tamil savory, like large nutty pretzels; *tikkiya*, potato cakes; *malai* chops, sweet sugary balls topped with cream; and almond-scented *pinnis*" (110). By contrast are the pick-up snacks

Theroux catches at intervals when the train chugs into a station for a brief stop to pick up or let off passengers. Then there is the fiasco at Sofia, back in Bulgaria, where long lines prevent his getting money converted and purchasing grub. Such disappointments of travel on public conveyances get chalked up to the luck of the draw.

The least engaging segment is dealing with Iran. It is there, though not exclusively, that Theroux becomes acquainted with *baksheesh*, a custom of bribes, giving tips to get the extras on trains and in hotels. Money talks in India, too, for beggars or to gain favors. Yet India is a kaleidoscope of shifting colors and contrasts. In reflecting on places to which he would not return, constructing a hypothetically shorter itinerary, he admits Iran is "penciled over, Afghanistan is deleted," and a few other places are marked "maybe" (294). However, India and most of the lands he visited would remain central.

On the train through India, Theroux hooks up with a Mr. Radia, whom he calls "the Anglophobe." Mr. Radia, his compartment mate, berates the Japanese and the English for their un-Indianness. He supplements the information about India that Theroux derives from other sources—his guidebook, Mr. Gupta of the Simla ashram, various professors, and other contacts he makes in the cities he visits.

Riding the *Rajdhani Express* to Bombay gives an eye-opening view of the city's sprawl. The approach to Bombay, riddled with slums, makeshift shacks, and remnants of cardboard and tin pieced together for partial shelter or, more simply, a floor or surface to sleep on, is telltale. Throughout India, its cities teem with the homeless and nearly homeless, the disabled and deformed, and the perpetually hungry, a portion of whom struggle to survive by begging, an omnipresent and pathetic gesture symbolic of the persistent failure of birth control. The trouble with India? The author pinpoints frankly: "There are too many Indians" (122). At a remote train station in Mathura, a village noted for its temple and sacred history, some miles beyond the populous city of Delhi (with three million strong and weak), Theroux is struck by the sight of a primitive tent village that had popped up on the platform proper: "They were spitting, eating, pissing, and strolling with such self-possession that they might have been in a remote village in the deepest Madrasa jungle" (115). Just as repulsive is the cook—not to be mistaken for a chef—on the train, who appeared as "a fat sweating Indian cook in filthy pajamas preparing vegetables for the pot by gathering them with his forearms and then slapping and squeezing them into a pulpous mass" (114). One recalls Chaucer's cook, who likewise turns off appetites. No wonder Theroux turns vegetarian for spells along the way.

In India, even in the densely populated areas, one is never far from animals—goats, monkeys, cattle, and beasts, all revered and allowed to wander everywhere. Among other vexing problems of human or animal origin is the hopelessness of preserving the country's valued artifacts: "On the ornate temple walls, stuck with posters, defaced with chisels, pissed on, and scrawled over with huge Devanagari script advertising Jaipur businesses there was a blue enamel sign warning visitors in Hindi and English that it was 'forbidden to desecrate, deface, mark or otherwise abuse the walls.' The sign itself had been defaced: the enamel chipped—it looked partly eaten" (125).

In Calcutta, where Theroux's companion, Mr. Chatterjee, a Bengali, serves as his guide, squatters are everywhere. They occupy premium empty space on train platforms, public places, doorways, and city pavements. Streets are congested with rickshaws and assorted vehicles: "wagons, scooters, old cars, carts and sledges and odd, old-fashioned horse-drawn vehicles." A close-up reveals a miscellany of contents: "In one cart, their white flippers limp, dead sea turtles were stacked; on another cart was a dead buffalo, and in a third an entire family with their belongings—children, parrot cage, pots and pans. All these vehicles, and people surging among them" (176). Pitifully, the scene in Calcutta is repeated across the urban landscape of India. As Mr. Chatterjee trenchantly and tersely puts it, "'Too much of people!'" (176)

As with any observant traveler, first impressions may remain, but they may also change and intensify as closer study accretes more detail and as time passes.

> On the first day the city [of Calcutta] seemed like a corpse on which the Indians were feeding like flies; then I saw its features more clearly, the obelisks and the pyramids in Park Street Cemetery, the decayed mansions with friezes and columns, and the fountains in the courtyards of these places: nymphs and sprites blowing on dry conches,

> who, like the people living under them in gunny sacks, are missing legs and arms; the gong of trams at night; and the flaring lamps lighting the wild cows pushing their snouts into rubbish piles, vying with the scrabbling Indians for something edible.

Starving people combing through garbage, "recycling ragpickers," disfigured and lame bodies—"in a city of mutilated people only the truly monstrous," the freakiest of the pathetic lot, "looked odd." Among the oddities is a man with one leg, "hopping . . . like a man on a pogo stick." That haunting image epitomizes India: "afterwards," notes Theroux, "whenever I thought of India, I saw him—hop, hop, hop—moving nimbly through those millions" (176).

Theroux experiences both the ugly and the beautiful. Another memory, a fonder one, is that of a romantic fling he has with a pretty Indian girl. Sirens and prostitutes wander the city streets wherever he visits in Asia, a temptation he resists whether in India, Singapore, Vietnam, Thailand, or elsewhere the red-light glimmers. One of Theroux's adventures takes him to Gokteik Gorge on a troublesome train ride from Rangoon to Mandalay via a side trip along the border of China. Despite rainy weather and a problem concerning his status as a foreigner, he is determined to see the engineering marvel, a grand viaduct arching over a chasm in the jungle with a swirling river far below and a series of tunnels to pass through on the way.

Like the linguistically perceptive narrator of *Gulliver's Travels*, the narrator here offers tidbits on the languages, dialects, and quirks of speech he encounters. He hears Tamils "babbling in that rippling speech that resembles the sputtering of a man singing in the shower" (131). English may be universal, but its rendering often borders on being provincial or unintelligible. For instance, "English is spoken in Malaysia in a nasal bark, a continual elision of words; phrases are spat and every word-ending is bitten. It is a pared-down version of English and sounds for all the world like Chinese until one's ear is tuned to it by the din of jungle sounds next to the track, the squawks of locusts and macaws, and monkeys cleaning their teeth on twanging strips of bamboo. This brand of English is devoid of every emotion but whispered hysteria" (226).

Quite a library emerges from the titles of books the narrator reads in his spare time and alludes to or quotes passages from in the text. Theroux, after all, is a man of letters. English authors cited are Shakespeare, Dickens, Browning, Trollope, Ruskin, Stevenson, Gissing, Forester, Conrad, Maugham, Joyce, Lawrence, and Greene. Names of Americans Poe, Twain, and Faulkner appear, and a host of classics and continental works make the list. Theroux carries an assortment of guidebooks with him and, along the way, picks up a few books, especially works by contemporaries in the lands he visits, such as *The Autobiography of a Yogi* and *Japanese Tales of Mystery and Imagination*.

In length, the catalog of trains rivals the bibliography. To look at the chapter titles is to see innumerable trains whiz by and to underscore the fact that the narrator's journey by rail summons many different lines. They run the gamut of services from none to first-class, cover terrain, and provide a potpourri of passengers of competing interest to the writer and, by extension, to those traveling via the book. Numerous stops occur along the way: to linger while a mechanical mishap is resolved, to let off or take on passengers and their baggage, and meanwhile to grab some food from a hawker, or, if the junction is on the itinerary, to get off and stay a while to explore the location, observing its people, features, and sights of architectural and historical significance. The ways of life of others become those of the traveler or are noted for later contemplation and inclusion in the resultant book of travel.

Theroux settles in for the long haul. "I had learned," he admits, "to become a resident of the express, and I preferred to travel for two or three days, reading, eating in the dining car, sleeping after lunch, and bringing my journal up to date in the early evening before having my first drink and deciding where we were on the map." He continues, "Train travel animated my imagination and usually gave me the solitude to order and write my thoughts: I travelled easily in two directions, along the level rails while Asia flashed changes at the window, and at the interior rim of a private world of memory and language. I cannot imagine a luckier combination" (166).

While indulging a stay as the sole guest in a luxurious Burmese hotel, Theroux dines and enjoys a drink and, except when interrupted by the waiter bringing him more good things to consume, leisurely reads a book. Self-reflectively, he confesses he falls into the category of travelers who enjoy "the journey only because of the agreeable delays en route, a lazy vulgar sybarite searching Asia for comfort, justifying my pleasure by the distance traveled" (198). Theroux notes how traveling, especially on a train, and writing affects one. One forgets everything and is lost in the activity and thought of writing. At such times travel isn't expanding one's outlook but instead causing one to retreat from it to carry out the task of reflecting upon aspects of it already over. The motif of a joyful, enthusiastic traveler is sustained except for an occasional trance-like lapse in which the traveler is diverted by the work of compiling grist for the manuscript of the travelogue. Near the end of the journey, he wants to surrender his seat on the train in exchange for the comforts and company at home.

The excitement, peculiarities, and cultural immersion offered by each train—its departures, stops, and amenities—are chronicled for the delight of the silent passengers on board via the book. Theroux writes glowingly of the State Railway of Thailand. He remarks,

> I knew enough of rail travel in Southeast Asia to avoid the air-conditioned sleeping cars, which are freezing cold and have none of the advantages of the wooden sleepers: wide berths and a shower room. There is not another train in the world that has a tall stone jar in the bath compartment, where, before dinner, one can stand naked, sluicing oneself with scoops of water. The trains in any country contain the essential paraphernalia of the culture: Thai trains have the shower jar with the glazed dragon in its side, Ceylonese ones the car reserved for Buddhist monks, Indian ones a vegetarian kitchen and six classes, Iranian ones prayer mats, Malaysian ones a noodle stall, Vietnamese ones bulletproof glass on the locomotive, and on every carriage of a Russian train there is a samovar. The railway bazaar, with its gadgets and passengers, represented the society so completely that to board it was to be challenged by the national character. At times it was like a leisurely seminar, but I also felt on some occasions that it was like being jailed and then assaulted by the monstrously typical. (209)

Theroux's jail term pays off, however, for both from the cell and out its windows, he extends his and his readers' breadth of experience and knowledge about the world beyond home, country by country. In

Singapore, Theroux discovers "a society where newspapers are censored and no criticism of the government is tolerated" (238). In Vietnam, Theroux witnesses lingering eruptions of Viet Cong violence, a population sprinkled with half-American babies, and a country that has become host to hybrids like American games, bits of the English language, and relics such as army uniforms and half-intact GI barracks. Yet "of all the places the railway had taken [him] since London, this was the loveliest" (259), he says of Danang. Saigon, "with the bars and brothels closed, . . . had the abandoned look of an unused fairground after a busy summer" (151). The traffic of soldiers, helicopters, and weaponry had died down, but in the aftermath, a stock of souvenirs from the war survived.

In Japan, Theroux buys clothes suitable for Siberia, his other clothes worn out after hours and hours of sitting on trains and not warm enough for the cold territory he would spend 6,000 miles crossing aboard the *Trans-Siberian Express*. The Japanese—with their slick bullet trains, luxury baths, studied courtesies, accommodation to crowded lines, and preference for pornographic films and comic books full of horrific violence—he identifies as "a people programmed" as if they "all have printed circuits" (271).

On the last and longest, northerly leg of the trip, Theroux enters snow country. On a voyage for part of it, crossing a lake linking railways, he encounters a section of Russia which, before the snows hit, is all "brown, flat, and treeless." He labels it "the grimmest landscape I had ever laid eyes on" (309). Subzero temperatures and heavy snowfall dominate the remainder of the trip through Russia, "the longest train journey in the world" (311). Necessarily, people viewed from the train window are bundled up in furs and padded dark coats and hats and boots, looking like beasts preparing for hibernation.

Indoors, unbundled and out of the frigid temperatures, they find contentment slugging vodka, a custom honored by the Russians he shares space with on the train. The clear liquor is taken as a remedy, something trustworthy to stir circulation and cope with the elements and the times. During a dull stretch through the Soviet tundra, Theroux admits, "Once I had thought of a train window as allowing me freedom to gape at the world; now it seemed an imprisoning thing and at times took on the opacity of a cell wall" (323). He sums it up: "Siberia was wood and snow" (327). It was all cedars and blowing snow along the borders of China and Mongolia. Replace with snow the water in Coleridge's *Rime*, in which water's potential to quench thirst and serve the purposes of navigation is gainsaid by the presence of salt and the absence of wind, and the scene transforms into that of Russia. "Another day, another night, a thousand miles; the snow deepened" (331). The trip achieves a welcomed highpoint when the Volga comes into view, and they reach Moscow at Christmas, though hardly soon enough for the rail-weary traveler. Carols playing on a compartment companion's radio tuned to BBC intensifies Theroux's homesickness. He exclaims, "I resented Russia's size; I wanted to be home" (339). Unluckily, he is still far from London, and visa problems delayed his return trip home for a few days.

His valedictory is that of a momentarily jaded traveler who is glad to have at least finished the course. Exciting as the wares, vendors, and sights and sounds of a bazaar may be, the curious visitor will surfeit after a time and wish to move on, coveting the silence of solitude, concluding that attractions have turned into distractions. Theroux has reached the climax of his journey and longs to disembark. He winds down:

> I slept through Warsaw, glared at Berlin, and entered Holland with a stone in my stomach. I felt flayed by the four months of train travel: it was as if I had undergone some harrowing cure, sickening myself on my addiction in order to be free of it. To invert the cliché, I had had a bellyful of traveling hopefully—I wanted to arrive. The whistle blew at level crossings—a long moronic hoot—and I was mocked by it, not bewitched. I had been right: anything was possible on a train, even the urge to get off. I drank to deafen myself, but still I heard the racket of the wheels. (341-42)

Retracing the route mapped out on his completed itinerary, in the way of a coda, he signs out: "All travel is circular. I had been jerked through Asia, making a parabola on one of the planet's hemispheres. After all, the grand tour is just the inspired man's way of heading home" (342). The book and the journey end full circle with the author repeating, but now in italics, the opening sentence of the book, a redaction of the four thick volumes of notes compiled en route. "'*Ever since childhood, when I lived within earshot of the Boston and Maine, I have seldom heard a train go by and not wished I was on it*'" (342).

In an earlier travel book, *The Kingdom by the Sea*, published in 1983, Theroux walks and catches buses and trains as he follows the jagged shoreline around Great Britain. He is nonchalant about—deliberately avoids—the customary sights, instead interested in experiencing and writing about whatever he encounters that tickles his fancy or upsets him or sheds light on the reality of the lives of the Brits. Often low-key, Theroux does not put on airs or praise what he deems unworthy, regardless if some find his criticisms offensive. For instance, looking at a map of the British Isles, he sees England, Scotland, and Wales suggesting the shape of a pig. For Theroux, in *The Kingdom by the Sea*, politics is a field to tramp into and root out the stubble and weeds. On a tramp or a train, Theroux is one whose journeys make for fascinating reading.

DARE TAKE *THE LUNATIC EXPRESS*?

Carl Hoffman's *The Lunatic Express*, published in 2010, carries the descriptive subtitle "Discovering the World . . . via Its Most Dangerous Buses, Boats, Trains, and Planes." Pressed against teeming humanity in all manner of vehicles and sleeping quarters, journalist Hoffman set out to travel four continents—the Americas, Africa, and Asia—using their respective public, often run-down and super-crowded conveyances. The repeatedly documented fact that the populously patronized modes of transportation were grossly overcrowded, often outdated, and notoriously dangerous was the lure for him. Early river voyages on the Amazon and a remote river in Peru consume a few weeks, but the total journey, during which he pretty much covers the globe, keeps him away from home and family and in foreign elements for nearly half a year. He logged many miles, withstood grueling conditions, and fought with dangers bordering on mayhem and ensuring inconvenience, novelty, and absence of privacy. While there were acquaintances back home who wrote him off as "nuts" or "masochistic," he felt he was "lucky" for the opportunity, recalling Thoreau, to "live deeply."

Hoffman delighted in living on the edge of disaster, traveling on ships and trains and buses that were replacements for their ruined predecessors, and viewing up-close lands and waters that had been scenes of warfare, fatal accidents, and epic disasters. Imbued with the spirit of a survivor and possessing the makeup of a daredevil, undaunted by harsh challenges and overwhelming odds, ready, even eager, to forego the advantages of civilized family life, he wanted to see and explore. Having separated from his wife recently, he welcomed the prospects of living differently, without the insulation peculiar to the fortunate but more like most of the world's population. As an intrepid journalist and traveler, he was drawn to the pleasure of interviewing persons and reconstructing past events, especially disasters involving passengers who happened to have survived a major wipeout on a train or ship.

At times Hoffman invokes the elegiac mode, so committed is he to reconstructing former events involving passengers who perished in a tragic train or shipwreck. He will go to great lengths to recover newspaper accounts and contact survivors he interviews to ascertain the details of the tragic event. The investigations don't eschew the morbid and the actuary and may entail a trip to the morgue. "Once I started seeing all those deathtraps out there, . . . I wanted to jump on and circumnavigate the planet on that unseen artery of mass transit. I wanted to know what it was like on the ferries that killed people daily, the buses that plunged off cliffs, the airplanes that crashed" (12). He wanted to face and endure the risks that others routinely faced. Such was the seed that sprouted the wayward journey he labeled "the Lunatic Express." As precautionary steps in setting out, he took emergency supplies, including an inflatable life vest, a high-powered flashlight, and medications. What appealed to him was the gamble of it and the adventure of trying on others' lives, straddling two worlds: the quotidian comfortable sphere at home and, by contrast, the exotic, dangerous realm elsewhere. He yearned to sojourn in truly foreign lands, to travel "via a series of veins and arteries that didn't show up on most of the developed world's anatomy charts" (34).

Hoffman's definition of foreign travel doesn't center on pleasure, at least as commonly defined. Rather, he emphasizes the fact that the traveler is certain to face danger anywhere and to a larger degree in less developed parts of the world, much of it issued from the public vehicles utilized, depending on their age and mechanical condition and the degree to which unsafe crowding of passengers occurred on them. Safety was also jeopardized by the bulk and weight of cargo crammed aboard. Of course, the ambient political climate and level of criminality in parts of the globe compound the level and frequency of danger to which outsiders and natives alike are subject. Hoffman confronts the problem head-on as a challenge, a stance others might interpret as foolhardy. He desires to partake as the people out there do and subsequently to share the results with his readers, the avid armchair travelers cruising in his wake and riding on the rails and roads he favors, however perilously in his journey. Hoffman doesn't preselect his guests or separate himself from the throng by resorting to first-class accommodations. He follows suit with the overwhelming array of humanity—eating and drinking no better or less, sharing crowded standing, seating, and sleeping arrangements, be they inconvenient and detrimental as long as they suffice and are available at low cost.

The first bus Hoffman hops aboard, departing from Chinatown in Washington, D.C., where he lives, is bound for Quebec. A short leg of his journey and headed somewhat out of the way; it is symptomatic of his plan to travel not in tourist style but with the hoi polloi and of his status as a father and husband who had recently checked out. He sought a new beginning by embarking on an odyssey that would test his independence and versatility and educate him about the wider world. As a journalist, he was trained to make and draw connections to create a story. This book is a tale of his daring to ride "The Lunatic Express."

After several preliminary travel-research gigs, Hoffman determined to set out "To experience travel not as a holiday, but as it is for most people: a simple daily act of moving from one place to another on the cheapest conveyance possible. A necessary part of life, like brushing your teeth or sleeping or making love" (8). Hoffman reminds us that the very word for *travel* is at root the very word for "work" or "toil." He points out that despite the widespread conception of tourism as a huge business or industry predicated on the pursuit of pleasure, for "*most* of the world's travelers," travel is "still a punishing, unpredictable, and sometimes deadly work of travail" (9). He became increasingly aware that commuting disasters across the globe occurred by the legion but escaped with little or no public notice beyond where they occurred. What sank in was that "On all those buses plunging off cliffs and sinking ferries and crashing planes, people were unself-consciously making arduous and unpredictable journeys every day" (12). Uncannily drawn to the danger zone, he felt compelled, excited, and enthusiastic to abandon home and join the fray. He started his escape mission, to which he admittedly became addicted, by electing to fly Cubana, an airline touting "one of the worst safety records in the sky." From Havana, as the sketchy outlines of his itinerary took shape, he would aim for Bogota and the peaks of the

Andes, thence to the heart of Africa, and next to the plateaus of Asia—all travel to be undertaken on vulnerable public conveyances with known reputations as deathtraps. Add to that the unsavory political climates encountered. For Hoffman, this fling with danger felt "oddly pleasant." Maybe it all was exaggerated. He'd see.

The larger half of the book, in terms of pages and time recorded, is centered on the journey through Asia. After a short break following the trip through Africa, Hoffman heads to Indonesia. Fittingly, he introduces the Indonesian segment by describing the enormous steel ferry *Siguntang*. Aboard the ferry, he feels "totally submerged in otherness." What could be more natural in that habitat? An archipelago of 17,000 islands held together by ferry boats crowded with passengers way beyond the declared unsafe limits, many sneaking aboard rather than coughing up the modest ticket price. Hoffman joined the crowd of commuters. His trick to gain sociability with natives was to do what they did: drink what water or other liquids they drank, adopt their toilet manners and use the primitive facilities available, eat when and what they ate, sit or lie and sleep shoulder-to-shoulder with them, in boats customarily on floors instead of beds, standing up jam-packed in trains. In short, he would go third class, third world! Through an astute study of the infrastructure of the less-developed countries and sections of the world, Hoffman gained firsthand knowledge and experience of their everyday modes of travel. The public conveyances tolerated minimal or mostly inadequate standards. As a participant in the transportation infrastructure, Hoffman was enabled empathetically to progress in his quest to identify the ways of those he was visiting and, importantly, temporarily living among.

In India especially, the trains were dangerous. Significantly, Mumbai hosted the most packed and dangerous trains in the world. At five a.m., on his way to the train station from his hotel in Mumbai and headed to drastically more crowded Bangladesh, Hoffman "threaded past rows of bodies wrapped in blankets and scarves lying on the sidewalk" (172). Aboard, "As the steel train clacked and shook and rattled and a man with a leg twisted at some impossible angle hobbled by on wooden crutches, I wondered what I was doing there" (175). He realized he was desperate to experience true friendship and "human warmth," but actually, "all alone rattling through India" and earlier, on jaunts to the Congo and elsewhere, what he gained in his isolation was not even a taste, much less a diet of new friendships and close human interaction. He was encountering overwhelming crowds and too rarely settling for mere passing acquaintance with fellow passengers, all packed on public transport vehicles and everywhere on the sidelines and in throngs defining the cities on his circuitous route. The epiphany, the inspiration to cultivate relationships, vitally changes his journey. It wins him unexpected and growing intimacy with those next to whom he is seated aboard ramshackle deathtraps and spaces of inconvenience. Riding the rails and waters in notoriously inadequate and irregularly survivable public contrivances offered the opportunity to bond with individuals and families traveling in similar circumstances. The success of Hoffman's travels, figuratively on the Lunatic Express, pivoted on a tug of war "between being connected and being separate, between being part of a group and being alone." His trial attempts at joining and participating in their company and family togetherness for uninhibited and extended periods became his modus operandi. Accepting the novelty of being regarded as a surrogate family member, he was fulfilled as a wanderer away from his former and competing roots and self-absorption.

Every portion of his journey tested his capacity for overcoming (while going out of his way to face) known dangers as he sought to fall in with the pattern of life among constituents. Bihar, "India's poorest state, with an illiteracy rate of nearly 50 percent [and] . . . rife with banditry, murder, suicide, road accidents, and corruption," despite or rather because of warnings, Hoffman "thought might be interesting to take the bus right through its midst" (201). It was too vast a project to see and comprehend everything. "The deeper I pushed," he acknowledged, "the harder it became to know them. . . . Each was a world unto its own that I could glimpse but never know" (198). He was buoyed by the enormity of the challenge.

To get around in the cities of Asia, Hoffman would typically rely on an auto-rickshaw, which choice frequently called upon him to be squeezed next to two or three others besides the driver. On the streets, he met and once in a while even engaged the services of an itinerant ear cleaner, shoe shiner, masseuse, or tout (one who hired out to help others shop), persons with whom he got intimately acquainted. Street life teemed with positive and negative realities. What a network of illegal stuff for sale to smoke, chew, or swallow! Drug lords, racketeers, and sales-pitchers aplenty everywhere. On the wholesome side, tea ceremonies vied with smoking customs for popularity. Markets offered heaps of farm produce and fresh fish.

He got used to it in no time and readily made a practice of traveling troubled buses, trains, and boats as he had vowed upon setting out. He depended on them for both the thrill and the necessary means of getting from place to place and for the chance to form companionships with strangers sitting or standing smack dab next to him. He had serious second and third thoughts about the sanity of his traveling "on the edge" in Afghanistan, the tensest of all his trials to stay safe and not get apprehended, kidnapped, or shot. But the conviction repeated in the account of his travels—his rationale for spending so much of his life in foreign lands apart from ties back home—was that "what travel was all about [was] showing you things in a starker way than you could ever see them at home" (235).

China exerted a barrier linguistically. He knew no Chinese but a couple of basic greetings and queries, which didn't work because he couldn't manage the pitch accurately. His teenage daughter emailed him an assortment of handy phrases, but again the accent failed him. It was "like trying to communicate with fish in the sea" (250).

The Lunatic Express assembles a unique chain of bus terminals, train stations, airports, wharves, and taxi and rickshaw stands and summons company with a host of commuters, mostly like him, traveling less than tourist class. While straightforwardly narrated, the itinerary is spontaneous, sometimes the next destination depending on the most readily available or adventurous option for getting there. There seemed always to be an array of potentially exciting or dependable modes of conveyance. Rarely does he pass up an impromptu side trip, such as the day and a half trip to Buro Island, offering a glimpse of life out of the mainstream. From Bogota, Ecuador, he picked Quito as his next destination "because it sounded good, and . . . would take me straight through Columbia." He'd go at night, which, because it was ill-advised on account of persistent guerrilla war activity, could be "more interesting." Top that with Latin American roads being among the most accident-prone in the world, with bus crashes steadily making up the statistics. On that rainy night bus ride winding through mountain roads sans guardrails, he and the bunch aboard got "a plate of steaming curried chicken and rice and cornmeal wrapped in a banana leaf" with their ticket. The connecting bus, following a coastal road and passing through market towns, featured a TV in front. From time to time, various vendors hopped aboard to peddle their wonderful pills, candy, sodas, corn on the cob, and other intriguing wares. The passengers could observe "a world of banana trees and cycads and thatch and sand roads" (33) and follow the panorama of the varying landscape. A half-day from Lima, they meandered via a run-down bus through the more remote territory, away from cities, and up into the Andes to penetrate a poor region some 450 miles distant.

A highlight of his South American visit was the invitation his eighteen-year-old daughter Lily accepted to fly out and accompany her father on this part of the trip that he particularly wanted to share. After dropping Lily off at the airport, he decided against La Paz, Bolivia, and the World's Most Dangerous Road—too touristy—instead set off by bus across the Andes to Puerto Maldonado, Peru, and then on to the border of Brazil by shared car. From there, he went by bus to Rio Branco, where he caught the ferry to Manaus. He elected not to take a ride on the so-called Train of Death. Avoiding the Transoceanic Highway, he next ventured forth aboard a 100-foot Amazon riverboat. The month on that continent ended with a flight to another—Africa.

The 600-mile railway track from Mombasa, Kenya, to Kampala, Uganda, constructed in the 1890s by Indian coolie labor, resulted in a death toll of 32,000 and won it the nickname of "The Lunatic Express," which Hoffman adopted for the title of his travel text. In India, he becomes a regular customer on "matatus," Kenya's ubiquitous minivans, with seating capacities ranging from 14 to 51 and reputations for speeding on unpaved roads by drivers accustomed to fighting off fatigue with drugs. They were rated "some of the most dangerous and crowded conveyances in the world" (81). The urban scene spoke of mass confusion. "Getting in and out of downtown Nairobi was five lanes of chaos, honking, and blue-black exhaust" (91).

Thankfully, Hoffman possesses both the journalist's esteemed skill of pursuing the right questions and the knack for getting acquainted and gaining personal and vocational knowledge from practically anybody in proximity. The stage he occupied starred among its dramatis personae a minivan driver, the guy shouldered up to him in an adjacent seat on a bus, a train, or a plane, and any number of persons occupying spots on the deck of a ferry or crammed into a crowded commuter vehicle or even a rickshaw. He soon adroitly knows many foreigners he meets, not just their names but their traits, habits, and family status. That's enough glue to affix details into a pattern or picture to populate the travelogue from point to point and achieve perspective. It helps that as narrator and guide, Hoffman commands and ably uses a vocabulary incorporating the correct semi-technical terms when needed, slang where it fits best, and a sweep of words varied and exacting yet colloquial in character and, when desired, downright chatty. Rarely is he either pedantic or strained in origin, trite, or vague. He explains the ins and outs of subjects and features encountered as he travels: the trade of bus drivers and the array of vocations met with at every turn. Those he engages with opine on a raft of local economic matters, such as fares, wages, and salaries people earn, and how burdensome their work is. Occasionally, they are responsible for a complaint, but mostly they come off as strikingly philosophical in viewing their circumstances, doubtless knowing they can't change or improve much in their immediate theater of action or influence. Topics zeroed in on include the unfolding landscapes traversed and, of course, the modes of conveyance. Add to the list the cost of services and meals and drinks, plus times when he is treated by a recent acquaintance, especially as he is asked in a friendly fashion about America and evident swindles and aspects of his family life. Perpetually in crowded conditions, Hoffman is grateful for little moments of privacy, such as when he manages to get a clean, silent hotel room: "It was an almost unspeakable luxury" (95).

Apart from the threatening circumstances constantly hovering over his journey and the intriguing panoply of vehicles conveying him and fellow passengers from place to place, what is so fetching about the travelogue is the style in which it is rendered. One aspect of the writing that pleases is the frequent resort to figurative language. As the author, Hoffman masterfully employs similes and metaphors, scores of them, as a seasoning to accentuate the meaning. In Peru, "people were so brown and withered they looked like canned mushrooms" (40). On spontaneity of expression, "when they found an appreciative listener, their stories could spill out with the force of a gusher of oil" (79). Describing crowded conditions, Hoffman writes, "at a semicircle packed with matatus [equivalent of taxis], like a thousand ants trying to squeeze into the same hole" (85). He conveys a claustrophobic sensation: "I leapt from the minivan as if I had been held under-water for too long" (95). To apprise the reader of woebegone sleeping conditions aboard a train, he offers a graphic comparison: "My mattress [on a bunk bed in a wreck of a train] was so stained it looked like a bullet riddled soldier had died on it" (103). The suffocating atmosphere he encountered is conveyed with an image: "Smoke from hundreds of cigarettes hung in the air like faded, yellowed lace curtains" (123). Describing a latrine break, he writes: "twenty-five men standing (or squatting) in a line like some grotesque Roman fountain" (203). To capture the bright beauty of a starry night: "stars sharp like strings of Christmas lights overhead" (230). To suggest the response to extreme temperature: "a line of shaking, freezing people jumping up and down like engine pistons" (249). So natural seems the spring from which he draws his similes. Wouldn't you agree?

The leg of the journey completed by train from Bamako to Dakar, which "was legendarily bad," sustained its reputation. Throughout Asia, there are grubby scenes galore and tableaus of the disabled, blind, dying, and destitute. Glancing ashore from a crowded boat, Hoffman reports, putting it metaphorically and with a burst of personification, "crumbling slums elbowed hard against the banks" (182). I don't know how many would choose to duplicate this journey in toto. But most of us would not want to miss arm-chairing this one.

A story wrapped within a story can intensify the latter. A haunting story encapsulated here revolves around the telling statistics of the passenger load in the case of the sinking of the ferry ship *Joola*. Besides the "1,046 officially ticketed passengers . . . at least another 717 had either bribed soldiers for passage or simply snuck on board" (115). The ship sailed its final voyage from Dakar six years before Hoffman's arrival. Its successor, the ship Hoffman planned to board the day after he alighted a train from Bamako, the *Diatta*, could now be gently tossing in the commemorative waves.

On deck, Hoffman met a chap named Zaid Zopol, a veritable polyglot whose girlfriend Amimata was tall, very attractive, and—at the prospect of sailing on the *Diatta*, particularly knowing she couldn't swim—very frightened. With Zopol's aid, Hoffman finagled to contact a certain Frenchman in charge of the organization of the ship's survivors and through him to get a person to interview to get the full account of the sinking. The survivor, Pierre Colly, a young athletic man, showed up and gave his interviewer the full scoop. He commenced by reporting that the mood aboard the *Joola* eerily recalled that of the *Titanic*. Inevitably, Colly soberly affirmed, the greatly exceeded maximum capacity of 580 passengers proved gravely detrimental, for such extensive displacement of water made navigating problematic in the rough weather coming up at the time. Burdened with an overload, the bulky craft listed. A sudden hard rain compounded the already compromised situation. A loud crack and accompanying jolt signaled the death knell. Colly heard and felt the alarm. The shifting weight caused the vehicles in the hole of the ferry to snap their chains, and the released freight caused the ship to roll, overturn, and sink. Passengers by the hundreds washed overboard. Helpless, most of them quickly floundered and drowned or froze in the cold, rough sea. Of the 1,863 confirmed passengers on board, only Colly and sixty others survived the death toll, including Colly's older brother. The tragedy of the *Joola* exceeded the recorded loss of the *Titanic*. This segment of the book is curiously and effectively a tale within a tale. Judging by the script, ably presented by the author of the enveloping travelogue, Colly proved an effective raconteur.

Other past disasters on public conveyances get mentioned, but none come as close to front-page coverage as the anniversary sinking of the *Joola*. As already observed, title page importance is reserved for the disastrous toll of fallen laborers incurred during the building of the so-called "Lunatic Express." Similarly, bearing the impact of a refrain, each chapter of the book is prefaced by a news release based on an accident resulting in multiple fatalities on another ferry boat, a bus, a minivan, a train, or an airplane. One could argue that any more emphasis here on fatal wrecks and the travelogue would switch genres and become chiefly a necrology or an elegy depending on tone and treatment. This way, it's a mix but still a tale of travel, one whose very title epitomizes tragedy emanating from a failed travel undertaking.

Unfolding through the book is an album or gallery of sorts, with verbal portraits of numerous persons met and gotten to know along the way. Many appear and are rendered close up for a page or more and then fade away for a spell before either disappearing altogether or reappearing in person or memory. Others stay around longer or crop up again at strategic points. Most are fleeting presences, certainly those making up the background or a crowd. But the close-ups suffice for filling out the time spent, and places stayed, however long or short. They help populate the ferry boats, trains, and buses that piece the work together and add life—and death—to the tale. Consider the sentence in which Hoffman is regarded as one of them: "In my space on my plank [his reserved place], I was an old family member [to those lying on the bed-less deck floor beside him]" (133).

Another album or gallery is created by descriptions of the ever-varying horizon, the panorama offered by the surrounding landscapes and seascapes as viewed by the occupants of the vehicles traversing the unfolding miles. A single swipe of the artist's brush will suffice: "A pod of porpoises sliced through the royal blue waves" or "whales spouted off the bus and their big flakes slapped the sea." Among structures noted are concrete buildings serving such purposes as warehouses, industrial enterprises, stores, and office headquarters. On a smaller scale, humble, one-room houses are inhabited by burgeoning families. Along the way, occasionally, evidence of conflict is shared: churches and mosques burned, isolated military action, occasional fights breaking out, crowd disturbances, and illegal acts being witnessed.

An express train takes Hoffman from Mumbai to New Delhi, where a terrorist strike killing 50 people erases his plans to stay with friends for a few days over Thanksgiving, but he's been left a note and directions to join others in their absence. The journey continues to Afghanistan, where Kabul and the surrounding area are under threat by the Taliban. A flight to China can't come fast enough. Following seven weeks in Bangladesh and Afghanistan, he lands in Urumqi on New Year's Eve. The trajectory of his trip is finally west and homeward. Puzzling out the next leg of the trip, bundled up but still shivering, he rides a tired bus through brown mountains before hooking a frigid 36-hour ride with two fellows taking turns driving a propane truck with no heater. That ordeal over, in Ulan Bator, a taxi bears him to the train station where he boards for Vladivostok on a piece of the Trans-Siberian Railway. The arrival in Russia, in turn, facilitates the coveted flight west to Los Angeles. There, rather anticlimactically, he hops on a Greyhound bus to spend four days and nights on the road, stopping at McDonald's for Big Macs and potty breaks and being nauseated by the too familiar route and trite bits of overheard conversations. The bus marathons it from Barstow to Vegas, Vail Pass, Kansas City, St. Louis, Pittsburg, and finally, Baltimore, where a blown tire prompts him to taxi to D.C. The last pages furnish a rolling coda of the journey, a wistful celebration of the unforgettable encounters and impressions uniquely defining "the Lunatic Express," a salute to the value of travel.

The Lunatic Express essentially earns the reader's interest and respect from its dovetailing of two features. Unforgettable is its depiction of the author's identification, acquaintance, and friendship with a wide spectrum of fellow travelers, disproportionately commuters-residents, whom he joins along the way. Simultaneously and equally memorable and galvanizing, is his recounting of the trip's emphasis on using modes of transportation that, while or even because they are over-crowded and obsolete, succeed in linking people to their various destinations, be they far or near, and to one another.

EPILOGUE

Just as a taste of travel can lead to a diet of travel, reading a single tale may entice one to read others. Often the company of a guidebook is welcome. It will ensure that in addition to the joy of spontaneous encounters with the new and different and the satisfaction of having completed bouts of obligatory sightseeing, the traveler—before or after, or even instead of, taking off—has the advantage of surveying the entire realm of possibilities. Equipped with a guide, the would-be traveler can work in or leave out options and put together a personalized, prioritized itinerary. Next time through, the guided traveler can choose where or what to omit or indulge, with only the price or trouble of fetching the book and expending the time it takes to read versus incurring the cost in real-time and what could amount to a considerable sum to go there physically rather than virtually.

One way or the other, tales of travel will take us there. Homer's world traveler Ulysses, in Tennyson's poem by that name, declares, "I cannot rest from travel." The Greek warrior's biography starts and ends with wanderlust. "Always roaming," he boasts, "Much have I seen and known—cities of men / And manners, climates, councils, governments. . . . I am a part of all that I have met." Having made a career of traveling, Ulysses is unstoppable. He intends to go out by way of a final triumphant voyage: "To sail beyond the sunset." Travelers on the seas and across the lands, whether they have gone there physically or by way of the imagination, feel a bond with fellow travelers. It is that bond that *Journey by the Book* seeks to celebrate and intensify.

Some travelers yearn to mingle with the famous, visit monuments, and make a genuine vacation out of the trip. Some light up at the prospect of sailing uncharted seas, island hopping, or seeking exotic ports of call. Others have in mind a journey that will put them in touch with interesting people, that involves stopping at unmarked, little-known places off the main road, or that offers an opportunity to enjoy the challenge of learning the language and history and discovering the idioms and the ins and outs of those whom they meet along the way. All categories of travelers know that the mode of travel they choose will likely govern what kind of experiences and memories the journey will create. Just as where they go and where they stay or linger may make or break the time spent away from home. Regardless, the tale of travel is what remains when the motion stops and reflection, the distillation stage of the journey, likely already begun while the travel is underway, takes over. Then a tale of travel is born. That is the best souvenir, the one worth sharing, the takeaway, a boon to the armchair traveler who, happy for its being well told, is curious to find out where you were and how it all turned out.

DESCRIPTIVE CONTENTS

INTRODUCTION

Journey by the Book: A Guide to Tales of Travel focuses on selected works in which a voyage, pilgrimage, or journey is central to the work's meaning and structure and in which the narrator and style attract and hold the interest of the reader. Targeted tales of travel are those distinguished by their descriptive and meditative quality, the presence of a continuous journey, and the dynamic rapport the narrator succeeds in establishing with the reader. While mode, method, destination, purpose, duration, and scope of travel vary with the individual author's experience and intention, all such factors related to the given itinerary conduce to shape the account of the journey and play a role in piquing the curiosity and satisfying the wanderlust of the armchair traveler.

STEINBECK'S AMERICA REVISITED: *TRAVELS WITH CHARLEY*

The itinerary of Steinbeck's *Travels with Charley* takes in the USA by region and favors out-of-the-way places. In a lively and reflective style, the book provides portraits of persons and places visited—the result of both planning and spontaneity. Dialogue and descriptions make for an intimate sketch of the country and a cross-section of its population. The author's voice, the style it is rendered, and the positive chemistry produced between the narrator and the reader raise the tale of travel above the category of mere travelogue. The novelist's discovery was twofold: while places of wilderness are still accessible, modern throw-away society has encroached conspicuously.

ERIC NEWBY'S MOCK-EPIC TALE: *A SHORT WALK IN THE HINDU KUSH*

Neither a short walk nor a trumped-up climb over a molehill, Newby's journey to Afghanistan to scale the 20,000-foot peak of Mir Samir tantalizingly makes little of much. The book covers a month of preparation for, hiking and climbing adventures in an isolated mountain range in Asia. Not one to boast or employ hyperbole except for humorous effect, Newby, a novice, chronicles in expanded diary mode the perils and obstacles to achieving a pipe dream, minimizing the dangers and defeats that befall him and his party. Snow, ice, dirt, sand, mud, rocky terrain, rivers, wind, and rain punctuate the itinerary. Challenges be gone; persist to the top!

TRAVELS OF MARCO POLO

Encyclopedic in thrust, Marco Polo's account of his travels and appointed missions to and within the near and far East purports to tell the truth. The case for its authenticity is attested to by including copious details and illustrations concerning exotic practices, fascinating places and unusual inhabitants, flora, fauna, teeming markets, and architectural marvels beyond Europe of the late 13th century. Full of contrasts and opinions allegedly informed by experience, the book is a treat for the armchair traveler yearning for an early report of emerging global ties.

SHIP AHOY: NAVIGATING *GULLIVER'S TRAVELS*

A classic of imaginary journeys, *Gulliver's Travels* is narrated by a resourceful narrator, who is an accomplished surgeon and seafaring Englishman and a stickler for details, many of which simultaneously astonish and create verisimilitude. The perspective shared in the four voyages allows the reader access to a worldview highlighting both the grossness and pettiness of human behavior and the ongoing difficulty of balancing reason and passion. The book springs from and excites wanderlust. It offers comic insight through the dynamic of a gullible narrator operating under the auspices of an author prone to satire. *Gulliver's Travels* resonates as a parody of scientific investigation, travel literature, and treatises designed to reform and perfect those whom Swift viewed as fallen creatures subject to pride and sorely in need of redemption.

FOOTPRINTS IN THE SAND: ROBYN DAVIDSON CROSSING THE AUSTRALIAN DESERT

Not as a caravan but as a solo event, Davidson, a young woman with a dream, succeeds in traversing the desert terrain of Australia. Arrestingly titled *Tracks,* her account pays vivid attention to the chosen pack animals, flora and fauna encountered, the monotony, beauty, and challenges that characterize the epic feat, and the toll the arduous journey takes on her selfhood. Interludes when an aboriginal guide joins her or a professional photographer interrupts her privacy to fulfill their mutual contract with *National Geographic* offset moments of suspense and drama when wild animals charge or when the traveler feels psychologically defeated and has to regain the stamina to carry on. The narrative, rendered in captivatingly lively prose, abounds in description and combines literal detail and figurative significance.

MARK TWAIN ABROAD

Twain's two travel works celebrating tours to Europe and the Middle East differ in scope and intent. *Innocents Abroad* is a full-blown survey in which the narrator is a guide not only supremely knowledgeable but adventurous and witty as well. *A Tramp Abroad* is a comic tour de force. Veering toward the mock-epic and always preposterous for the sake of being preposterous, the tales that comprise the volume published a decade later than *Innocents* encompass comic fiascos aplenty. From a farcical duel between cowards that ends bloodlessly to an assault on the Alps by a pseudo-ceremonial expedition, the discovery that one can climb a mountain effortlessly by telescope, and a critique of the awful state of the German language, the book is hilarious in its deflation of high-flown claims. All are narrated by pilgrim Twain in the company of his sidekick Mr. Harris, both resisting the "tramp" implied in the book's title and each ostensibly determined to pick up on art, culture, and the German language.

FOLLOWING IN BUNYAN'S FOOTSTEPS: *PILGRIM'S PROGRESS*

Through allegory and dream, the structure and appeal of *Pilgrim's Progress* are age old. A tale of travel on foot, the pilgrimage of Christian from the city of destruction to the celestial city, is a journey full of challenges, from traversing rough terrain to fighting monsters and being on guard lest fellow travelers retard his and Faithful, his sometime companion's advance toward the "wicket gate" en route to the golden destination. The figures along the way, whose identity is evident in their tag names and the daunting landscape, whose contours and geographical features bespeak metaphorical significance, contribute to the reader's suspense over whether Christian will adhere to the "straight and narrow" path, the same pilgrimage Christian's family makes in the second part of the book. The language, albeit somewhat archaic, often smacks of the idiomatic. The dialogue, frequently turning to catechism but not without the flow of good gossip, speaks to the spiritual issues at stake while adding grist to the characterizations. The tale forms an archetype of the Christian life through its itinerary and landscape.

JUPITER CIRCLES THE EARTH

Simon's worldwide trip on a motorcycle, *Jupiter's Travels*, is an epic journey consuming four years and toting up 65,000 miles. In the company of the narrator, the reader vicariously experiences a variety of climates, conditions, peoples, and wildlife from Egypt to Australia, South and North America, and the East, covering forty-some countries. Not just a "kaleidoscope of scenarios," the trip affords the narrator opportunities for intimate involvement with persons he meets and leads to a compassionate encircling of the weary of the planet. Simon concludes "that the interruptions *were* the journey." The style is animated, and the language is brimming with figurative flourishes. This tale of travel is hard to beat for sheer adventure, bounty of information, detailed tailoring of characterization, build-up of suspense, moments of introspection, power of description, and orderly presentation.

HOMER'S *THE ODYSSEY*

The ancient Greek epic finds its hero triumphant only at the end of a decade of huge obstacles, the aftermath of his return from victory in a battle of ten years' duration. The episodes involve the gods, who impede and assist him on his homeward voyage. He is held captive on an island by a goddess, outwits a Cyclops, and contends with sea monsters and storms that wipe out his entire crew but is befriended by the Phoenicians and the goddess Athena to safely harbor in Ithaca, where father and son vanquish the greedy suitors and Odysseus is happily reunited with his long-suffering wife, Penelope. The journey motif and the storytelling dynamic combine to make this a tale that fascinates now as it has over the ages.

A TRIP INTO THE CONGO: PENETRATING THE *HEART OF DARKNESS*

Conrad's mouthpiece and surrogate explorer, Marlow, reaches the interior not only of the Congo but that of the human heart, confronting the lure of greed and malicious power as incarnated in the legendary figure of Mr. Kurtz. The frame of the story, told to a cadre of professional men aboard a sailboat on the London riverfront, engages the reader as a spellbound listener and assists in extending the moral implications of imperial exploitation and the fall of man from a civilized to a savage state. The fall of humanity, while personified by Kurtz, is the potential fate of all. Kurtz is "the emissary of light" who survives the jungle but succumbs to the temptation to rule the natives as a god, only to acknowledge "the horror" of it all on his deathbed, leaving Marlow to serve as his executor. The journey is both Kurtz's and Marlow's and, as well, the journey of all humans trafficking in evil disguised as good.

GUIDE TO KEROUAC'S *ON THE ROAD*

Sal, the narrator's quest for thrills on the road westward, draws the reader into the trip's enchantment and the psychedelic moments that free the travelers from the restraints of conventional life and morality. By the close of the book, or journey, the heroic figure of Dean Moriarty is tarnished as Sal registers the failure of care he discovers in the madcap Dean. Till then, the engagement in parties, fast driving, heavy drinking, sex, drugs, begging, borrowing, and stealing to keep going is addictive, as are the reflective moments staring at the stars overhead and the enjoyment of genuine laughter and freedom of expression characteristic of the "gone" gang. The intended spontaneity of the text and the universal theme of a quest carry the book beyond the topicality of the vehicles on the road, the slang of the era, and the defining details of the beat generation. The goals of the trip are ever tied to anticipation more than realization, to the movement westward more than the arrival at a destination city or event.

NAIPAUL'S ISLAMIC JOURNEY

In recounting his extensive travel among the Islamic peoples, most of whom reside remotely from the geographical origin of their Muslim faith, Naipaul pays close attention to the tenets, practices, and attitudes of its adherents. He pierces to the core of a belief that holds to the letter of the law, seeks to overtake all impediments in ascending over all rival believers, and surrenders to a narrow vision of human freedom. The narration of the tales becomes the key source of pleasure and illumination for the reader. The journey explores the nooks and crannies of Islamic beliefs and delineates aspects of the lands and peoples who occupy those lands and who observe, not all uniformly, the rules prescribed in the *Koran*.

COLERIDGE'S *RIME OF THE ANCIENT MARINER*

In reading Coleridge's imaginary, dreamlike poem of the *Ancient Mariner*, one embarks on a real and fantastic voyage, a journey during which the mariner's spiritual thirst is kept unquenched until, spontaneously, under the moonlight, he gives way to compassion for all creatures. He can pray at that climactic moment, and the ship resumes its course under supernatural powers. Here again, the device of the frame serves to heighten the tale's dramatic intensity and underscore the theme of confession and penance, with which spiritual emphasis the tale gains universal impact both on the mariner as well as on those whom he compulsively tries to instruct by telling his own story of sin and redemption.

THINK AND RIDE AT THE SAME TIME: *ZEN AND THE ART OF MOTORCYCLE MAINTENANCE*

In *Zen and the Art of Motorcycle Maintenance*, the account of a motorcycle trip west from Minneapolis to San Francisco, Pirsig mounts a philosophical quest for Quality. Simultaneously, he attempts to piece together fragments of his past persona, whom he dubs Phaedrus. The geographical aspect of the journey pales by comparison with the reverie over the past, which haunts him like a ghost and is complicated by a relentless pursuit to achieve a balance between the romantic and classical modes of understanding and a resolution to the question of a mental crisis that cut short his teaching career and domestic stability. The shift from the level of surface activity to the higher level of metaphysics is accommodated by the mechanism of what Pirsig calls Chautauqua, a variation of internal monologue.

ADVENTURES ON THE HIGH SEAS: SAILING THE *KON-TIKI* AND *ROUND THE WORLD* WITH CAPTAIN COOK

Two very different voyages—that of Thor Heyerdahl, involving the sailing of a balsam raft from Peru to the Easter Islands, and the second fact-finding voyage of Captain Cook, as retold by naturalist George Forster—expand the reader's global knowledge and provide seaworthy adventure. The success of each tale arises from the respective narrator's descriptive and storytelling powers. How each tale is told is more important than simply the story being told.

BRYSON'S EXPANDED WORLD: *A WALK IN THE WOODS*

In *A Walk in the Woods*, Bryson supplies humor, social and institutional criticism, and scientific and geographical scope. He and his pal, both challenged by age and sedentary lifestyles, cover by foot but a fraction of the Appalachian Trail, yet it is enough to satisfy them that they had attempted and did complete in good faith a feat few Americans undertake. And it is enough to convince the reader of the grandeur, legendary status, and imminent dangers encapsulated in a primitive national park or forest. In stark contrast to the sweaty idyll of a working holiday are the glut of unwholesome fast foods, the infestation of tawdry shopping malls lurking just beyond the perimeter, and the deplorable depletion of woods and species for which the nation is to blame. The point of view and the lavish, steadily funny descriptions, narrations of episodes, and characterizations of the few hikers they encounter along the way combine to make the journey worth reading.

DANA "BEFORE THE MAST"

Dana's *Two Years Before the Mast* is more than a log by a landlubber and college student turned seaman. It does trace the transformation from novice to a veteran sailor. But it also portrays the experience of voyaging on a commercial sail-rigged vessel, the saga of acquiring, transporting, and trading cargo, and the test of physical and moral stamina to withstand the demanding work aboard and ill-treatment by bully captains, and the off-setting splendor of rare free time ashore and the bond of intimate friendships. The book documents and celebrates the coming of age and the melding of physical and mental challenges.

TRAVELING *BLUE HIGHWAYS*

William Heat-Moon's *Blue Highways* opens to view a variety of niches of America's regions and their galleries of genuine personalities. His tale is real for the sure and insightful guidance he gives in shaping the itinerary and for the versatile management of the narrative evident in a style ranging from the vernacular to the learned—smooth shifting of gears desirable in any vehicle. Vignette after vignette, the book situates the reader as if in earshot and sight of the places and persons visited. The bond with the narrator makes for a comfortable ride through the byways of Americana, catching once standard or uniquely eloquent scenes before they vanish.

ON THE RAILS WITH PAUL THEROUX

Paul Theroux narrates from the rails, the reader assuming the posture of a fellow traveler and gawker in a kaleidoscopic journey across the vast distances and varying continental identities of Europe and Asia. Variety aplenty, as in a bazaar, the book splurges on images of haunting indelibility: disabled limbless beggars, the opinionated and the official, field laborers and petty administrators, beautiful girls and grubby passengers, countryside plush and wasted, gorgeous and hostile. The mode of travel defines the vision. Scenes out the train's window, events occurring inside, and episodes of encounters when alighting to explore a place and meet representatives of diverse cultures and climes—the miles of the track become the ticket for the reader to travel afar and see and understand and question much. Throughout, the narrator is the reader's companion and escort, both avid observer and genial host. The book ends with a coda and an expression of the homesickness that inevitably settles in on a trip strung out for a long time, covering great distance, moving from the familiar to the foreign, and ultimately returning to the familiar. Such is the trajectory of many a journey.

DARE TAKE *THE LUNATIC EXPRESS*?

Spurning the customarily convenience-oriented tourist's trip abroad and instead yearning for an experience akin to that of the world's masses, who have no option but to patronize a raft of notoriously unsafe and annoyingly crowded public conveyances, journalist Carl Hoffman shares a vivid account of a half-year spent on what he intriguingly calls "The Lunatic Express." He is unabashedly drawn to the dangerous, relatively cheap modes of travel by the thrill factor. Yet he sees the transportation system, albeit a mixed bag, as fundamentally instrumental for achieving his mission: to explore the globe and familiarize himself and his prospective readers with the plight, aspirations, and traditional ways of common citizens worldwide, as borne out by the many whom he meets and gets to know, ardent commuters ungrudgingly making ends meet. Hoffman's is an exceedingly unusual and absorbing tale of travel.

EPILOGUE

Just as a taste of travel can lead to a diet of travel, reading a single tale may entice one to read others. The tale of travel is what remains when the motion stops and reflection, the distillation stage of the journey, likely already begun while the travel is underway, takes over. Then a tale of travel is born.

ACKNOWLEDGMENTS

My digitally-savvy daughter and unofficial project manager, Abby, deserves credit for successfully rocketing my manuscript into orbit and subsequently, with equal magic or sleight of hand, launching a volley of supporting satellites with documents on board that helped expedite its publication. In conversations over the years, my son Nathaniel, an insatiable and perceptive reader, shared many insights relevant to the contents of my emerging book, so much so that *Journey by the Book* would otherwise have been thinner and less pointed in its claims and breadth of observations. He was the first to turn the pages and draw my attention to a raft of books: Beamish, *The Voyage of 'the Cormorant,'* Bryson, *The Lost Continent*, Hoffman, *The Lunatic Express*, and McMurtry, *Roads*. My wife Rhoda's close reading of many of the works cataloged and explored in *Journey by the Book* intensified the benefits of conversations about them that sprang up over the period of the book's composition. I have profited handsomely, too, because she is a wordsmith of the first water. In countless classes and syllabi over the years, my students served as an enthusiastic sounding board and laboratory for the testing and infusion of ideas related to a broad range of literary topics, including many tales of travel. During the phase of seeking permissions from publishers to quote copyright material, I received personal emails from Bill Bryson and Carl Hoffman, reinforcing the collegiality shared by academics and writers the world over. For the metamorphosis from manuscript to release stage, I greatly appreciated the careful editing by Abigail Henson and the steps taken by Lawrence Knorr, CEO, Taylor Berger-Knorr, Assistant to CEO, Joe Walters, Marketing and Publicity Coordinator, and Crystal Devine, Coordinator of Book Design, whose expertise and work as members of the team at Sunbury culminated in the successful launch of *Journey*.

PRINCIPAL WORKS CITED

Brown, Christopher K. *Encyclopedia of Travel Literature*. Santa Barbara, CA: ABC-CLIO, 2000. Print.

Bryson, Bill. *A Walk in the Woods: Rediscovering America on the Appalachian Trail.* 1998. New York: Anchor-Random, 2007. Print.

———. *The Lost Continent: Travels in Small-Town America.* 1989. New York: Perennial-Harper, 1990. Print.

Bunyan, John. *The Pilgrim's Progress.* 1678. Mineola, NY: Thrift-Dover, 2003. Print.

Coleridge, Samuel Taylor. *The Rime of the Ancient Mariner and Other Poems.* 1798. Mineola, NY: Thrift-Dover, 1992. Print.

Conrad, Joseph. *Heart of Darkness.* 1902. Mineola, NY: Thrift-Dover, 1990. Print.

Dana, Richard Henry Jr. *Two Years Before the Mast: A Personal Narrative of Life at Sea.* 1840. New York: Classics-Barnes, 2007. Print.

Davidson, Robyn. *Tracks.* 1980. New York: Random House, 2014. Print.

———. *Desert Places.* New York: Penguin Books, 1997. Print.

Forster, George. *A Voyage Round the World* [In His Britannic Majesty's Sloop, Resolution, commanded by Capt. James Cook, during the Years 1772, 3, 4, and 5]. 1777. 2 vols. Eds. Nicholas Thomas and Oliver Berghof. Honolulu: U of Hawai'i, 2000. Print.

Fussell, Paul, ed. *The Norton Book of Travel.* New York: W.W. Norton, 1987. Print.

Heat-Moon, William Least. *Blue Highways: A Journey into America.* Boston: Houghton, 1991. Print.

Heyerdahl, Thor. *The Kon-Tiki Expedition: Across the South Seas by Raft.* 1950. Trans. F. H. Lyon. New York: Simon, 1973. Print.

Hoffman, Carl. *The Lunatic Express: Discovering the World . . . via Its Most Dangerous Buses, Boats, Trains, and Planes.* New York: Broadway, 2010. Print.

Homer. *The Odyssey.* Trans. Robert Fagles. New York: Penguin, 1986. Print.

Kerouac, Jack. *On the Road.* 1957. New York: Penguin, 1999. Print.

"The Literature of Travel, 1700-1900." *The Cambridge History of English and American Literature in 18 Volumes.* Vol. XIV. New York: Putnam's, 1907-21. *Google Book Search. Web.* 7 Sept. 2009. *<bartleby.com>*.

Naipaul, V. S. *Among the Believers: An Islamic Journey.* 1981. New York: Vintage-Random, 1982. Print.

———. *Beyond Belief: Islamic Excursions Among the Converted Peoples.* New York: Vintage-Random, 1998. Print.

Newby, Eric. *A Short Walk in the Hindu Kush.* 1958. Oakland: Lonely Planet, 1998. Print.

Pirsig, Robert. *Zen and the Art of Motorcycle Maintenance: An Inquiry Into Values.* New York: Bantom, 1974. Print.

Polo, Marco. *The Travels of Marco Polo.* Trans. Ronald Latham. New York: Penguin, 1958. Print.

Simon, Ted. *Jupiter's Travels.* 1979. New York: Penguin, 1980. Print.

Steinbeck, John. *Travels with Charley: In Search of America.* 1962. New York: Penguin, 1980. Print.

Swift, Jonathan. *Gulliver's Travels.* 1726. Mineola, NY: Thrift-Dover, 1996. Print.

Theroux, Paul. *The Great Railway Bazaar: By Train Through Asia.* 1975. Boston: Mariner-Houghton, 2006. Print.

———. *The Kingdom by the Sea: A Journey Around the Coast of Great Britain.* 1983. New York:

Penguin, 1984. Print.

———. *The Tao of Travel: Enlightenments from Lives on the Road.* London: Hamish Hamilton Harcourt. 2011. Print.

———. *The Tao of Travel.* New York: Houghton Mifflin Harcourt, 2011. Print.

Toynbee, Arnold. *East to West: A Journey Round the World.* New York: Oxford, 1958. Print.

Twain, Mark. *The Innocents Abroad: or the New Pilgrims' Progress.* 1869. Mineola, NY: Thrift-Dover, 2003. Print.

———. *A Tramp Abroad.* 1880. Mineola, NY: Thrift-Dover, 2002. Print.

PERMISSIONS

Excerpts from *A Walk in the Woods: Rediscovering America on the Appalachian Trail* by Bill Bryson, copyright © 1977 by Bill Bryson. Used by permission of Broadway Books, an imprint of Penguin Random House LLC, and by permission of Anchor Canada/Doubleday Canada, a division of Penguin Random House Canada Limited. All rights reserved.

Excerpts from *On the Road* by Jack Kerouac,_copyright © 1955, 1957 by John Sampas, Literary Representative, the Estate of Stella Sampas Kerouac, John Lash, Executor of the Estate by Jan Kerouac; Nancy Bump; and Anthony M. Sampas. Used by permission of Viking Books, an imprint of Penguin Publishing Group, a division of Penguin Random House LLC. All rights reserved.

Excerpts from *The Lunatic Express: Discovering the World . . . Via Its Most Dangerous Buses, Boats, Trains, and Planes* by Carl Hoffman, copyright © 2010 by Carl Hoffman. Used by permission of Broadway Books, an imprint of Random House, a division of Penguin Random House LLC. All rights reserved.

Excerpts from *Tracks* by Robyn Davidson, copyright © 1980 by Robyn Davidson. Used by permission of Vintage Books, an imprint of Random House LLC, a Penguin Random House Company, and by permission of Bloomsbury Publishing. All rights reserved.

Excerpt from *The Odyssey* by Homer and Translated by Robert Fagles, copyright © 1996 by Robert Fagles. Used by permission of Viking Penguin, a division of Penguin Books USA Inc. All rights reserved.

Excerpts from *Travels with Charley: In Search of America* by John Steinbeck, copyright © 1961, 1962 by The Curtis Publishing Co.; copyright ©1962 by John Steinbeck copyright renewed © 1989, 1990 by Elaine Steinbeck, Thom Steinbeck, and John Steinbeck IV. Used by permission of Viking Press, an imprint of Penguin Publishing Group, a division of Penguin Random House LLC.

Excerpts from *Blue Highways: A Journey into America* by William Least Heat-Moon, copyright © 1982. Reprinted by permission of Little Brown, an imprint of Hachette Book Group, Inc. All rights reserved.

Excerpts from [Capt. Cook's] *A Voyage Round the World* by George Forster, ed. by Nicholas Thomas and Oliver Berghof, copyright © 2000. Reprinted by permission of the University of Hawai'i Press.

Excerpts from *A Short Walk in the Hindu Kush* by Eric Newby, copyright © 1958 by Eric Newby. Used by permission of HarperCollins Publishers Ltd.

Excerpts from *Beyond Belief: Islamic Excursions Among the Converted Peoples* by V. S. Naipaul, copyright © 1981 by V. S. Naipaul. Reprinted by permission of Penguin Random House LLC and Vintage Canada, a division of Penguin Random House Canada Limited. All rights reserved.

Excerpts from *Among the Believers: An Islamic Journey* by V. S. Naipaul, copyright © 1981V. S. Naipaul. Reprinted by permission of Penguin Random House LLC and Vintage Canada, a division of Penguin Random House Canada Limited. All rights reserved.

Excerpts from *Zen and the Art of Motorcycle Maintenance* by Robert M. Pirsig copyright © 1974 by Robert M. Pirsig. Used by permission of Harper Collins Publishers.

Excerpt from *The Lost Continent* by Bill Bryson copyright © 1989 by Bill Bryson. Used by permission of Harper Collins Publishers.

Note: Quoted matter from two additional copyrighted works (Thor Heyerdahl, *Kon-Tiki*, translated by F. H. Lyon, 1973; and Ted Simon, *Jupiter's Travels*, 1979), totaling fewer than 300 words each, is within the realm of fair use.

ABOUT THE AUTHOR

Daniel E. Van Tassel is the author of Back to Barron, a chronicle of growing up in small-town-and-rural mid-century America. He graduated from St. Olaf College and earned his M.A. and Ph.D. degrees in literature from the University of Iowa.

He taught at Pacific Lutheran University, California State University San Marcos, and, for over two decades, Muskingum College, where he served as academic dean and professor of English. His scholarly publications include articles on Shakespeare, Hardy, Lawrence, and Beckett and numerous book reviews in *Modern Fiction Studies.*

Retired and living in Northfield, Minnesota with his wife Rhoda, he now teaches courses in the Cannon Valley Elder Collegium program. Subjects in his syllabi these days range from Humor, Poetry, Thomas Hardy, Chaucer, and Shakespeare to American Nature Writers, particularly Thoreau, Leopold, and Carson.

For recreation, he takes to trails daily on his mountain bike. In addition to reading, he enjoys participating in local theater, swimming, home restoration and decorating. Current interests remain centered on travel literature, architecture, and ecology, especially as manifested in climate change and endangered species.

The past ten years he spent writing and revising a manuscript now published as *Journey by the Book: A Guide to Tales of Travel.*

www.ingramcontent.com/pod-product-compliance
Lightning Source LLC
Chambersburg PA
CBHW011201090426
42742CB00032B/3393